In this issue

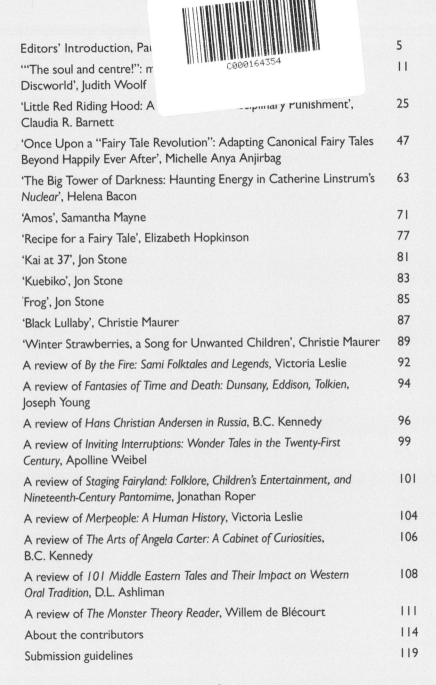

Editors' Introduction

For too long – certainly since *Gramarye 18* – it has felt like we have been living through a Narnia-like season in which it is always Covid Winter but never Christmas. But now, with various vaccines available – and new variants aside – it may be that we are stumbling towards a type of Yuletide. And lo, from out of the woods emerges Covid Father Christmas, bearing *Gramarye 19*.

In this volume Judith Woolf makes the case for the literary qualities of Terry Pratchett through a penetrating analysis of mortality and death in the Discworld novels. Claudia R. Barnett analyses changing perceptions of Red Riding Hood, with a particular focus on punishment and violence against women. The result is a riveting and detailed discussion of society's ongoing and evolving relationship with the girl in the red cap. Michelle Anya Anjirbag provides a wide-ranging review-cum-examination of the revision of canonical fairy tales undertaken by Vintage's Fairy Tale Revolutions series. Jeanette Winterson's *Hansel and Greta*, Rebecca Solnit's *Cinderella Liberator*, Kamila Shamsie's *Duckling*, and Malorie Blackman's *Bluebeard* all demonstrate ways in which the fairy tale can engage with contemporary politics and societal issues while moving the form beyond the conventional 'happy ever after' ending.

Gramarye's book reviewers have been busy during the various 'lockdowns' of the last six months and we have a bumper selection of books to tempt to you to stay at home for a bit longer or read while huddled in an isolation booth in a pub or restaurant. Victoria Leslie reviews a revived version of Barbara Sjoholm's *By the Fire: Sami Folktales and Legends* and finds a fascinating glimpse into the female world of the Talma and the Kareesuando Sami, and their feminine story-telling tradition. The book represents an important contribution to folklore studies by an overlooked pioneer of Scandinavian story collecting.

Joseph Young reviews Anna Vaninskaya's study of Dunsany, Eddison and Tolkien, *Fantasies of Time and Death*. With caveats around the discussion of Dunsany, Young nonetheless finds much to commend in this work, with its central focus on cosmogony and eschatology as recurrent ideas in the work of Tolkien and his now frequently overlooked predecessors in the fantasy genre. B.C. Kennedy discovers the joys of 'Anderseniana' in *Hans Christian Andersen in Russia*, a collection of essays which address the relationship between Andersen and Russia, and between Russian culture and Andersen from the 1840s until today. Apolline Weibel enjoys being lost in the woods of Cristina Bacchilega's and Jennifer Orme's *Inviting Interruptions: Wonder Tales in the Twenty-First Century*, which sees the fairy tale transformed and reinterpreted in a multimedia, format-defying reading experience. Jonathan Roper has a somewhat frustrating experience with Jennifer Schaker's *Staging Fairyland: Folklore, Children's Entertainment, and Nineteenth-Century Pantomime* but enjoys the pantomime images contained within the volume while acknowledging the value of the book in highlighting the link between page and stage in terms of fairy tales in the 19th century, thus demonstrating to an international readership the importance of the pantomime as a medium through which Victorians interacted with fairy tales.

Victoria Leslie returns to a perennial favourite topic of *Gramarye* when reviewing Vaughn Scribner's *Merpeople: A Human History*. Scribner's study addresses a millennium of accounts of merpeople – with a focus on the figure of the mermaid – demonstrating the 19th-century peak of mermaid-fever before moving the discussion into a modern setting in which the fluid nature of the merperson makes them a figure redolent of contemporary conversations about the nature of identity and gender. B.C. Kennedy reviews a second collection of essays, this time on the multidisciplinary interests of Angela Carter. *The Arts of Angela Carter: A Cabinet of Curiosities* includes discussion of a wide range of topics with which Carter engaged in her fictions, including topography, anthropology, religion, painting, and cinema.

D.L. Ashliman reviews Ulrich Marzolph's *101 Middle Eastern Tales and Their Impact on Western Oral Tradition* and discovers a 'timeless collection of tales' which operate as both a selection of stories with which to entertain an audience but also a critically rigorous collection which addresses the changes wrought in the migration of the tales from the East to the West. Finally, Willem de Blécourt provides a bracing, historically and critically informed review of *The Monster Theory Reader*. Monsters beware, the reviewer bites back.

· ·

Paul Quinn

Writing just over a year since the start of the first UK lockdown, with over 150,000 people lost to the pandemic, and still under a government that followed 'it will be over by Christmas' with 'there was never a PPE shortage' and – despite the clearly disproportionate impact of the virus on people of colour – 'there is no evidence for institutional racism in Britain', I am tempted to focus this introduction on the theme of clown-punched dystopias. Or at least Pinocchio. But as the submissions bag produced no obvious responses to the pandemic – not surprisingly, as many writers are still finding it difficult material to creatively transform – I will attempt instead, in honour of spring, a reflection on survival, resurrection and new growth. As Jon Stone's chillingly wise 'Kai at 37' puts it: after a searing encounter with the Snow Queen, 'What can you do but learn to love again?'

That's not to overstate the daffodils. Though anyone reading this has physically survived the virus (hopefully without lasting effects), Britain is still pulling between the Scylla of economic devastation – devouring jobs, livelihoods and entire retail chains – and the Charybdis of Covid-19, which, despite the vaccination programme, still has the potential to overwhelm the NHS. But lockdown is only one of Scylla's six heads: any sustainable response to mass unemployment must also tackle Brexit, robotisation, endemic historic inequalities, climate crisis and mass extinction. The alternative, as Samantha Mayne warns in her discreetly spectacular short story 'Amos', is to risk a ruined planet, scarcity, surveillance and regimentation, the damp, grey ambience of a 'formless drizzle' in which peace is indistinguishable from war. Those of us who are jabbed and hold pandemic-proof jobs have a responsibility to row as hard as we can in the direction of a country worth living in. I look forward to publishing work in *Gramarye* that responds to this terrible time with grief, anger, encouragement and vision; but for now teaching creative writing during the pandemic has convinced me that nurturing the critical imagination is in itself of great value. Writers of fairy tales, fantasy and speculative fiction are always charged with doing essential cultural work.

Take Scylla and Charybdis. The phrase flings monstrous froth over rocks and hard places, but when stirred the Greek myths – as so often – prove to reveal deep fears of women's sexuality. Charybdis – meaning 'sucker down' – was the 'voracious' daughter of Gaia and Poseidon;[1] for the crimes of stealing oxen or helping her father flood land, she was hurled by Zeus into the sea to become a flippered creature or 'never-sated' whirlpool.[2] Scylla – 'she who rends' – is a young woman pursued by a lustful god; in the various versions of her legend she escapes to a well or sheltered bay, only to be punished by a goddess who throws magic herbs into her bathing water. In *The Odyssey* Scylla is an oddly quiet barking six-headed monster with eighteen sets of teeth,[3] while in Ovid, as Judith Kazantzis observes, her metamorphosis is tragically incomplete: 'her lower parts were transformed into a clump of ravening dogs' heads extended on the ends of long haunches [and] she helplessly hid her human upper part in the cave, from which the

Dogs of Skylla rushed out to pick off passing sailors.'[4] Modern female poets from Kazantzis to Fiona Benson have often chosen to critique the misogyny of the Greek myths, and at a time when rape culture is now openly challenged, this work remains vital. But it is also important to face the collusion of jealous goddesses in the abuse of young women. In this issue, in fairy tale renderings that faintly echo Skylla's fate, Christie Maurer examines, with lyrical restraint, women's emotional violence against women. In 'Winter Strawberries, a song for unwanted children', a daughter retreats from her mother into a cold cove for comfort. In the more subliminally gendered 'Black Lullaby', a speaker caught between a 'high window' and the skirts of a 'drunk sea' withholds affection from a 'forgotten sister'. While one might still discuss 'cruel mothers' in the political context of immense domestic pressures on women, sometimes literature must simply be a fractured vessel for inexpressible emotion.

I'm sorry: did I say this introduction was going to celebrate spring? Let me hop then, to Jon Stone's complex and subtle responses to Japanese mythology. In 'Frog', Basho's famous splash ripples out into video gaming, Greek mock-epic verse and roadkill, generating – well, perhaps not crocuses, but a poem that seizes life from imminent death, and in so doing recalls the perennial vitality of mind expressed in the classic haiku. In 'Kuebiko', a concussed trickster figure offers a vision of a world as depressing as an Adam Curtis documentary: 'the way it all matters, but doesn't; is plotted, but isn't.' Hints of hope arrive, though, in the form of spells, stories, lies and a distant open door: ambiguous reminders that, in the human psyche, facts are always subject to the power of the imagination.

So, no daffodils at all, I'm afraid. But as we enter a summer of uncertainty, as Elizabeth Hopkinson reminds us in her delightful recipe, thanks to hazelnuts, golden goose eggs and helpful witches, there is always the delicious pleasure of the fairy tale, made to be shared on Rule of Six picnics. I will leave you to decide which Englishman to bake in your cake!

. . . .

Naomi Foyle

Notes

1. William Smith (ed.), 'SCYLLA and Charybdis' in *Dictionary of Greek and Roman Biography and Mythology*, vol. III, (London: John Murray, 1849), 762.
2. Virgil, *The Aeneid*, translated by Robert Fagles (London: Penguin, 2006), 3.497.
3. Scylla's soft yelp associates her, according to Robert Graves, with 'the white, red-eared death-hounds, the Spectral Pack or Gabriel Ratches of British legend, which pursue the souls of the damned … ancient Egyptian hunting dogs, sacred to Anubis, and still bred on the island of Iviza, which when in pursuit of their quarry make a 'questing' noise like the whimper of puppies or the music of the migrating barnacle goose'. Robert Graves, *The Greek Myths II* (London: The Folio Society, 1996), 659.
4. Judith Kazantzis, *The Odysseus Poems: Fictions on the Odyssey of Homer* (Hove: Waterloo Press, 2010), 37.

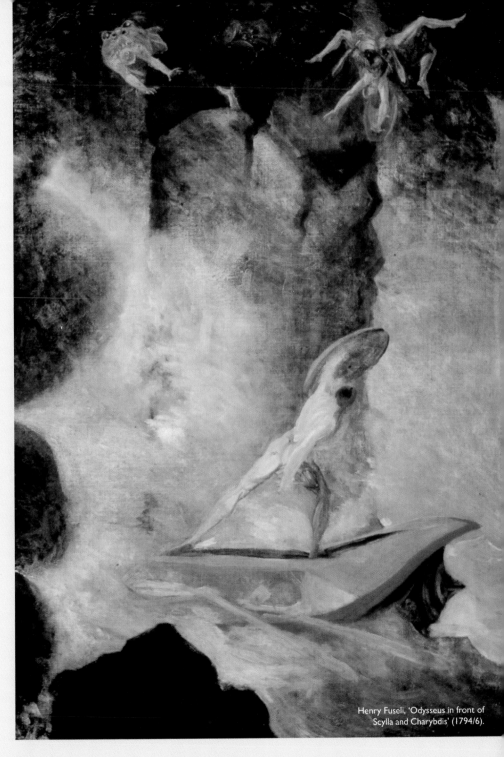

Henry Fuseli, 'Odysseus in front of Scylla and Charybdis' (1794/6).

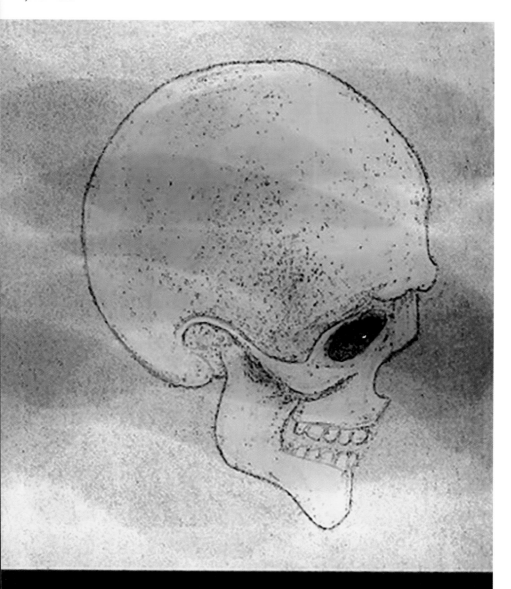

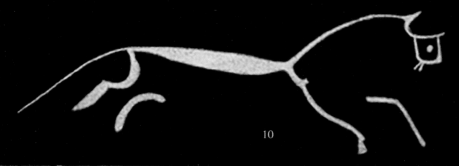

'The soul and centre!': morality and death in Terry Pratchett's Discworld

Judith Woolf

T
erry Pratchett's invention of an essentially secular universe (though one with more than its fair share of small gods) enabled him, as a convinced humanist, to explore the nature of moral imperatives in a world without the certainty of an afterlife, a project lent a new urgency in his final novels by his own terminal illness. On Discworld, where 'all metaphors are potentially real',[1] Death really does have a door, and even before cruel necessity made him a campaigner for the right to die, Pratchett wanted us to discover that the desert of black sand on the far side of it is not something we should fear. In his 2010 Richard Dimbleby lecture, *Shaking Hands with Death*, in which he used his early-onset Alzheimer's disease as the starting point for a powerful defence of assisted dying, Pratchett spoke (through his 'stunt Pratchett', Tony Robinson, since he was no longer able to read his forceful words aloud) about his first encounter with the personification which gave rise to his most popular character.

> When I was a young boy, playing on the floor of my grandmother's front room, I glanced up at the television and saw Death, talking to a Knight, and I didn't know very much about death at that point. It was the thing that happened to budgerigars and hamsters. But it was Death, with a scythe and an amiable manner. I didn't know it at the time, of course, but I had just watched a clip from Bergman's *Seventh Seal*, wherein the Knight engages in protracted dialogue, and of course the famous chess game, with the Grim Reaper who, it seemed to me, did not seem so terribly grim.[2]

Sometimes, if only in obedience to the law of averages, life really does imitate art. By the time he gave his Dimbleby lecture, Pratchett was himself a knight facing death, and one who thought of the terminal stage of his illness, in which posterior cortical atrophy would develop into full-blown dementia, as 'the endgame'. In the event, though his life was cruelly cut short, the endgame was relatively brief: it was only in his last few months that words finally failed him, preventing him from completing the autobiography on which he had embarked too late. After his death in March 2015, his daughter wrote that her father 'had done something with more success than anyone else – he made Death friendly', and described the 'tear-inducing letters from fans who were nearing the end of their lives and took great comfort in imagining that the death that came for them would be riding a white horse called Binky'.[3] 'Those are the kind of letters', Pratchett himself wrote, 'that cause me to stare at the wall for some time …'[4]

While few novelists can claim the power to console readers on their deathbeds, Pratchett's apparently cheery spin on Bergman's Reaper helps to explain why his fictive universe has seldom received the respectful critical attention accorded to Philip Pullman's *His Dark Materials*. However, if we look more closely at Pratchett's engagement with Bergman's dark portrayal of death and religion in *The Seventh Seal*, we will discover that the Death of Discworld provides him with a comic mask behind which deeply serious concerns can be explored. Bergman's film is predicated on the assumption that audiences will share the existential terror which leads the Knight to declare that if God does not exist, as Death slyly suggests to him, 'then life is an outrageous horror. No one can live in the face of death, knowing that all is nothingness'.[5] Pratchett's genial humanism was underpinned by a moral rage against oppressive thought systems no less intense than the passionate atheism which fuels Pullman's Miltonic war against Milton's God, and his motto was *Noli Timere Messorem* (Do not fear the Reaper). His fundamental opposition both to the idea that death should be regarded as a source of terror, and to those who seek to deploy that terror to frighten others into belief or conformity, provides much of the ethical scaffolding of Discworld.

Pratchett's admirers sometimes suggest that he was 'his generation's Dickens',[6] since what A.S. Byatt has memorably described as 'his squirming and insanitary metropolis Ankh-Morpork'[7] is in many ways a fantasy version of Dickens's London, not least in the scope it offers for parodic but keenly targeted social satire. Like Dickens, Pratchett crafted his novels to appeal to as wide an audience as possible. Readers in search of a thoroughly entertaining, and ultimately comforting, version of human life (in all its dwarf and troll and werewolf disguises) can immerse themselves in the story while relishing its lively comic wordplay. Others, including Byatt herself, read his narrative on two levels, recognising, beneath the apparently light-hearted verbal surface, the ingenious reframing of powerful, pre-existing story material by a writer 'whose wit is metaphysical'[8] and who, 'like TS Eliot's Webster, has always been much possessed by death'.[9] Pratchett himself said that Discworld 'borrows from folklore and mythology, twisting and tangling it on the way'.[10] To describe this as intertextuality risks sounding like a Lecturer in Recent Runes, not least because much of what Pratchett called white knowledge – the songs and stories and sayings and superstitions which, in theory at least, everybody knows, and which Shakespeare drew on before him – did not originate on the printed page.

Pratchett was, of course, as prodigiously productive as Dickens, but with the difference that every Discworld novel potentially adds to the backstory of those that follow, enabling him to tackle progressively darker and more ambitious themes. In the opening book of the series, *The Colour of Magic*, 'the Discworld – world and mirror of worlds'[11] is the literary equivalent of a fairground mirror, mockingly distorting the stereotypes of post-Tolkien fantasy fiction. However, in his later novels it offers a sharply focused view of the world it reflects – our world, with its challenges and moral dilemmas – though it is a view which only readers open to the creative possibilities of genre fiction are able and willing to see.

The art critic Jonathan Jones, having grudgingly read a single Pratchett novel, *Small Gods*, after being taken to task for dismissing as not worth reading an author he admitted to never having read, shrugs off the unwelcome experience: 'In the real world, as opposed to the Discworld, people have complexities, contradictions. A whole art form has evolved to explore them. It's called the novel.'[12] Pratchett was already dead when Jones delivered this high table put-down. A novelist who has been knighted for services to literature and given an honorary professorship by Trinity College Dublin needs no defending, but it is tempting to imagine what that most complex and contradictory of literary characters, Granny Weatherwax, might have had to say about it. Jones claims in his article that although, like Salman Rushdie, whose *Satanic Verses* was published four years earlier, Pratchett 'is taking on religion and seeking to undo fixed truths', he is merely 'mocking a non-existent faith and risking the wrath of imaginary fundamentalists'. But, as Pratchett himself pointed out, the premise of *Small Gods* is one which 'you would think would offend practically every religion' – that an established church risks becoming so powerful that 'there is really no more room in it for its god'.[13]

Unlike Pullman's all-powerful Magisterium, the Church of Om is fated to dwindle into a schismatic evangelical sect even less influential than the Nine Day Wonderers. In *Carpe Jugulum*, the novel Jones ought to have moved on to had he not decided to limit his reluctant engagement with Discworld to a single text, Pratchett uses the Church of Om to thread a vigorous debate about religious faith and doubt through his central narrative, in which the Lancre witches take on a suave family of invading vampires. When we overhear the troubled priest of the latter-day Omnian church, Mightily-Praiseworthy-Are-Ye-Who-Worship-Om Oats, singing snatches of a hymn he learned as a child – 'burn, with a clear bright light'[14] – the echo of Susan Warner's well-known 19th-century hymn for children, 'Jesus bids us shine / With a pure, clear light',[15] works as a bitter reminder that Christianity, a monotheistic religion originating at a time and in a place very similar to the Omnia of *Small Gods*, once caused human beings to be burned alive. In 16th-century England, heretics died at the stake under both Protestant and Catholic regimes. In Omnia, too, as in post-reformation Britain and the America of Warner's puritan ancestors, it was religion that fuelled the witch hunts. Although, like its real-life counterparts, the Church of Om no longer consigns witches or heretics to the flames, Mightily Oats himself – demoralised by his failure to live up to the injunction, of which Warner's hymn is a nursery version, to 'let your light so shine before men that they may see your good works'[16] – is haunted by his knowledge of its early history. With his mind 'split in half' by the struggle between faith and doubt, he is left uneasily aware that his appeal to the 'infinite compassion' of Om is only too open to question: '[W]hat compassion? How many people prayed at the stake?'[17]

Carpe Jugulum, along with *Maskerade*, the previous book in the series featuring the witches of Lancre, is one of the two novels in which Pratchett directly references *The Seventh Seal*. Oats, who has arrived in Lancre as a hapless missionary, echoes the plea of Bergman's Knight, who has returned home to a land ravaged by plague and questions why it should be 'so cruelly inconceivable to grasp God with the senses': 'I want knowledge, not faith, not suppositions, but knowledge. I want God to stretch out His hand towards me, reveal Himself and speak to me.'[18] Oats, too, 'has hoped that, just once, Om would make himself known in some obvious and unequivocal way that couldn't be mistaken for wind or a guilty conscience. [...] It wasn't that he'd lacked faith. But faith wasn't enough. He'd wanted knowledge.'[19] But, unlike Bergman's Knight, he tries to lay aside his inner struggle in the face of the threat menacing an entire community: 'Right now he'd settle for a reliable manual of vampire disposal.'[20]

Pratchett, as a schoolboy, had been horrified by the Old Testament, which he read in its entirety, and enthralled by Darwin's *Origin of Species*. 'By the time I was fourteen,' he wryly remarked, 'I was too smart for my own god.'[21] But although, as a humanist, he 'would rather believe that we are a rising ape, not a falling angel', he nevertheless retained 'a sneaking regard for the Church of England and those I disagree with. We should always debate ideas that appear to strike at the centre of our humanity. Ideas and proposals should be tested.'[22]

Oats's adversary in the debate about religious faith is the redoubtable Granny Weatherwax, who in *Maskerade* had herself taken on the role of Bergman's Knight, playing a poker game against Death (which he lets her win) for the life of a child, and in *Lords and Ladies*, published in the same year as *Small Gods*, had given a practical twist to the philosopher Koomi of Smale's theory that gods, large and small, 'come into being and grow and flourish *because they are believed in*'.[23] 'I ain't against gods and goddesses, in their place. But they've got to be the ones we make ourselves. Then we can take 'em to bits for the parts when we don't need 'em any more.'[24]

One of Pratchett's strengths as a novelist is that he never allows his central characters to harden into mere consistency. In *Carpe Jugulum*, Granny Weatherwax's anguished struggle with her own inner darkness allows her to speak with a new authority which at times is anything but comic. In *Maskerade* she had told Death:

> 'I have faith.'
>
> REALLY? IN WHAT PARTICULAR DEITY?
>
> 'Oh, none of *them*.'
>
> THEN FAITH IN WHAT?
>
> 'Just faith, you know. In general.'[25]

Now she makes terrifyingly clear to Oats the true price of the religious faith which he should be grateful that she lacks.

> 'Now, if I'd seen him, really there, really alive, it'd be in me like a fever. If I thought there was some god who really did care two hoots about people, who watched 'em like a father and cared for 'em like a mother ... well, you wouldn't catch me sayin' things like "There are two sides to every question," and "We must respect other people's beliefs." You wouldn't find me just being gen'rally nice in the hope that it'd all turn out right in the end, not if that flame was burning in me like an unforgivin' sword. And I did say burnin', Mister Oats, 'cos that's what it'd be. You say that you people don't burn folk and sacrifice people any more, but that's what true faith would mean, y'see? Sacrificin' your own life, one day at a time, to the flame ...[26]

Warner's injunction to shine 'Like a little candle/ Burning in the night' has been transmuted into Hugh Latimer's 'we shall this day light such a candle', leaving Oats abashed at his own insufficiency as she warns him not to chase the faith he will never catch. Then, 'almost as an aside', she offers him a way forward: 'But, perhaps, you can live faithfully.'[27] At the end of the novel she sends him a gift which once again takes us back to Warner's hymn: a jar in which a phoenix feather burns 'with a clear, cool light'.[28] Warner's 'In this world is darkness' applies to Discworld too, and Granny Weatherwax knows how much Oats will need this cool, illuminating clarity as he travels 'into dark places'.[29] The god who will keep him safe on his journey, though, will not be Om. As Pratchett told Mark Lawson in the BBC's *The Big Question*:

> The advantage that Discworld has got, which is not shared by what we are pleased to call the real universe, is that it quite genuinely has a caring god, which is to say, me. And I see to it that on the whole the good, or at least the less bad, win, or at least don't lose by too much, at the end of the book.[30]

This certainty that the narrative, for all its twists and turns, will eventually arrive at a happy ending – for, as Pratchett himself would say, a given value of happy – is another reason why critics often dismiss his fiction as escapist, sometimes even in the belief that they are defending it. Rupert Godwin in *The Times* notes that 'Pratchett's multi-dimensional frolics, spiced with esoterica, common-sense and sympathy, will never be taken entirely seriously. But then joyous escapism has always annoyed the intellectuals.'[31] (It is worth pointing out that the 'tell-tale compression'[32] of Jane Austen's pages seldom elicits the same response.) Nevertheless, in his novels as in his life, Pratchett does not shrink from exploring that darkest of dark places which he represents in the Discworld books as a desert of black sand under a dark but star-studded sky. The popularity of the richly comic and deliberately larger-than-life figure of Death gives him the freedom to talk about death with a lower-case 'd', confronting his readers with questions which are not asked lightly. What, if anything, lies beyond the black desert which on Discworld, where 'all metaphors are potentially real', stands for the unknown darkness which rounds all mortal lives? How should we deal with those lived experiences which occur before and after the unknowable moment of death: with dying and with grieving? What constitutes a good death, and, more crucially, in a universe without either a heaven or a hell, what constitutes a good life, and is there any forgiveness for an evil one? And do we agree with Granny Weatherwax that, at 'those times when medicines didn't help and headology was at a loss because a mind was a rage of pain in a body that had become its own enemy, when people were simply in a prison made of flesh', she was right to 'let them go'.[33]

The answer in the early novels to the question of what happens after death is that it all depends on the beliefs of the person dying. So in *Mort*, an elderly witch turns into the beautiful young woman she has always seen herself as being, before fading away 'like a Cheshire cat only much more erotic',[34] while a venerable abbot returns to the womb for his 54th reincarnation. However, as life on the Disc begins to reflect life on Earth more closely, death on the Disc needs to do the same thing. Pratchett saw himself as being 'in the unenviable position of someone that doesn't believe in a god of any sort but that thinks there may be such a thing as an immortal soul',[35] and this paradoxical mindset, together with his repurposing of Bergman's Reaper, gives him an original way of exploring the nature of mortality.

The Death of Discworld offers few clues to the newly dead, but in *Small Gods* he answers the question, 'What is at the end of the desert?' with the single word 'JUDGEMENT'.[36] In the closing pages, Brutha, the humble novice whose capacity for 'tolerance, compassion, charity, steadfastness and faith'[37] will lead to his becoming the human saviour of the Omnian church, recognises that this is a riddle, and solves it by asking, '*Which* end?'[38] However, both General Fri'it and Private Ichlos have earlier found their own solution by remembering the words of an old song: '*You have to walk a lonesome desert … You have to walk it all alone …*'[39] Pratchett adapts Woody Guthrie's version of the gospel song *Lonesome Valley* to fit the geography both of Omnia and of the desert of black sand, while retaining all of its haunting power. Fri'it, who has fought desert campaigns, suddenly finds himself able to think clearly:

> There were no lies here. All fancies fled away. That's what happened
> in all deserts. It was just you, and what you believed.
>
> What have I always believed?
>
> That on the whole, and by and large, if a man lived properly, not
> according to what any priests said, but according to what seemed
> decent and honest inside, then it would, at the end, more or less,
> turn out all right.[40]

Having discovered that the hell promised by the Omnian church is a fable, and passed the test of self-judgement, he sets out across the sand. For Ichlos, it is even simpler, since 'he was far less sophisticated than General Fri'it, and took more notice of the songs he'd learned in his childhood. Besides, he had an advantage. He'd had even less religion than the general.'[41] It is only on Vorbis, the fanatical head of the Quisition, that Death's riddle has the same effect as the doorkeeper's answer in Franz Kafka's ominous parable, Before the Law. Unable to be alone with himself, which would require him to recognise the source of his obsessive cruelty and accept responsibility for its hideous consequences, he is reduced, for a hundred years which pass like infinity, to a hunched figure paralysed with fear. He has to wait for the coming of Brutha, whose own nature makes him incapable of denying pity even to the tortured soul of a torturer, to begin his uncertain journey across the desert.

The most comprehensive answer to the question of what lies beyond it is offered in A Hat Full of Sky by young Tiffany Aching, who has entered Death's door while still alive to enable a hiver, an ancient disembodied entity which has attempted to possess her, to find the peaceful end it longs for. To learn how to die, it needs a unitary self, so she calls it Arthur, the name which the title of Thomas Malory's La Morte d'Arthur indissolubly associated with death. When the newly mortal Arthur asks her what is on the other side of the desert, she gives the reply of someone who does not subscribe to any religion, is keeping an open mind on whether there is 'such a thing as an immortal soul', and has no problem with living 'in the face of death' while accepting the possibility 'that all is nothingness'.

> Tiffany hesitated. 'Some people think you go to a better world,'
> she said. 'Some people think you come back to this one in
> a different body. And some think there's just nothing. They
> think you just stop.'
>
> And what do you think? Arthur asked.
>
> 'I think that there are no words to describe it,' said Tiffany.
>
> Is that true? said Arthur.
>
> 'I think that's why you have to cross the desert,' said Tiffany.
>
> 'To find out.'[42]

Although she is afraid of being permanently trapped between life and death, Tiffany has no fear of the tall, skeletal figure of Death himself. She knows that bones 'were only chalk that had walked around'.[43] Granny Weatherwax, who opens a door for her back into the living world, tells her, 'I know this path already. You'll tread it again, no doubt, for some other poor soul, open the door for them as can't find it'.[44] At the moment of Granny Weatherwax's death, in his final novel, *The Shepherd's Crown*, Pratchett makes this point again, now with the weight of his own mortality and his campaign for assisted dying behind it:

> Her visitor was no stranger, and the land she knew she was going to was a land she had helped many others to step through to over the years. For a witch stands on the very edge of everything, between the light and the dark, between life and death [...] Sometimes they need to help some poor soul through the final hours, help them to find the door, not to get lost in the dark.[45]

In his Dimbleby lecture, Pratchett was very clear about how he himself would choose to 'shake hands with Death': sitting on his lawn at home with Thomas Tallis on the iPod and a glass of brandy in his hand 'to wash down whatever modern version of the "Brompton Cocktail" … some helpful medic could supply'.[46] And he was very clear, too, about how his father would have died 'if there had been any justice or even narrative sensibility in the universe': at the moment when 'he suddenly looked up and said, "I can feel the sun of India on my face," and his face did light up rather magically, brighter and happier than I had seen it at any time in the previous year'.[47] Since Discworld 'quite genuinely has a caring god', Pratchett gives a version of that imagined good death to the Baron in *I Shall Wear Midnight*, who dies transformed by a joyful childhood memory into a little boy in an itchy tweed jacket smelling of wee, his face lit up by September sunshine and the flames of the stubble field where the hare ran into the fire and was not burned. It is typical of Pratchett that he adds a serious footnote to the Proustian comic detail of the jacket, explaining that 'The old cloth-makers used urine as a mordant for the dyes used in making woollen clothes, so that the colours would be fixed and not run'.[48]

It is said that a tragic actor can only play tragic parts but a comic actor can play anything, and as a great comic writer, Pratchett was good at portraying grief. In the Tiffany Aching novels, the last three of which were written during the campaigning and creative final years in which he lost both his parents and endured the gradual depredations of a disease which 'slips you away a little bit at a time and lets you watch it happen',[49] Pratchett casts 'a cool, clear light' on death, bereavement and burial. In *Wintersmith*, he gives the solemnity of a funeral pibroch to the lament that Awfully Wee Billy Bigchin, traditional bard of the Nac Mac Feegle, plays on his mousepipes (still with the little ears attached), standing on Miss Treason's grave.

> Humans could not hear the mousepipes very well because the notes were too high, but Tiffany could feel them in her head. A gonnagle could put many things into his music, and she felt sunsets, and autumns, and the mist on hills and the smell of roses so red they were nearly black ...
>
> When he had finished, the gonnagle stood in silence for a moment, looked at Tiffany again, then vanished.
>
> Tiffany sat on a stump and cried a bit, because it needed to be done. Then she went and milked the goats, because someone had to do that, too. [50]

In *The Wee Free Men*, when she found her grandmother dead, and knew that 'the world had ended',[51] the seven-year-old Tiffany had been unable to cry.

> *She'd felt coldness spread through her. It even had a sound — it was like a thin, sharp musical note. It had a voice, too. Her own voice. It was saying: It's too late, tears are no good, no time to say anything, there are things to be done ...* [52]

Now she has learnt what tears are good for. In *I Shall Wear Midnight*, when Roland, the Baron's son, who has been turning his anger at his father's death against her, mutters, 'Can you take away this grief?', she quietly replies, 'I would not do so even if I knew how. *It belongs to you.* Only time and tears take away grief; that is what they are for.'[53] But, as Nanny Ogg shows her at the Baron's funeral, the right song is needed too. The song the Baron's father had sung on that long-ago September day had a special significance for Pratchett, as he told Ginny Dougary in an interview about his documentary on assisted death, *Choosing to Die*.

> On the day that he was diagnosed with Alzheimer's, he was out in the garden singing (he demonstrates, and has a mellifluous steady voice): "Tis pleasant and delightful on a sweet summer's morn/ To see the fields and the meadows all covered in corn/ And the small birds are singing on every green spray/ And the larks they sang melodious at the dawning of the day."[54]

As Nanny Ogg cajoles a crowd of strangers into 'harmonizing like a choir', 'Tiffany wept, and saw through the tears a little boy in his new tweed jacket that smelled of wee, walking with his father under different stars'.[55]

What constitutes a life well lived in Pratchett's fictive universe is harder to define, not least because the two characters who might be seen as its moral guardians, Sam Vimes and Esme Weatherwax, are as angry, obstinate and driven as each other. They act as mentors rather than role models, Vimes to his younger self in *Night Watch* and to Feeney Upshot in *Snuff*, and Granny Weatherwax, after Pratchett brings her back at the end of *The Wee Free Men*, to Tiffany Aching. When it comes to the cardinal virtues, neither of them has any time for prudence, and though Vimes, the reformed alcoholic, certainly has need of temperance, it is only in the Victorian sense, while Granny Weatherwax takes austerity to a deliberately intimidating extreme. Her bare cottage is described in *A Hat Full of Sky* as 'the house of a life peeled to the core'.[56] For both of them, it is justice, and the fortitude necessary to defend it, which are of paramount importance. Vimes impresses on Feeney that 'no policeman swears allegiance to the civil power, he swears allegiance to the law,'[57] and Granny Weatherwax tells Mightily Oats that 'Mercy's a fine thing, but judgin' comes first. Otherwise you don't know what you're bein' merciful about.'[58]

As for the theological virtues, Granny Weatherwax, as we have already seen, has a capacity for faith, even if mainly in herself, and thus also for hope, but her crucial lesson for Tiffany is the importance of charity in its practical modern sense:

> It's sittin' up all night with some poor old man who's leavin' the world, taking away such pain as you can, comfortin' their terror, seein' 'em safely on their way [...] then going home and sitting down for five minutes before some shouting *angry* man comes bangin' on your door 'cos his wife's havin' difficulty givin' birth to their first child and the midwife's at her wits' end [...] *That* is the root and heart and soul and centre of witchcraft, that is. The soul and centre!' Mistress Weatherwax smacked her fist into her hand, hammering out her words. 'The ... soul ... and ... *centre!*'[59]

The inhabitants of the Chalk have their own moral guardian, Tiffany's dead grandmother, the shepherd who never lost a lamb. The overarching presence of Granny Aching illustrates Pratchett's belief that 'one thing that certainly survives is the outer soul of a person'.[60] A woman of few but effective words and the unerring ability to temper mercy with justice, she too has a lesson for Tiffany: 'Them as can do, has to do for them as can't. And someone has to speak up for them as has no voices.'[61]

As Tiffany grows into her vocation and takes on the task of caring for the vulnerable and the voiceless, she discovers for herself that justice and mercy can sometimes be two sides of the same coin. She cuts down the wretched Mr Petty, who has tried to hang himself after beating his pregnant 13-year-old daughter so hard that her baby was stillborn: 'here was a man one breath away from death. She had no option, no option at all. She had to give him that breath, for the sake of a handful of nettles.'[62]

The stinging weeds which Petty has arranged as funeral flowers around the little corpse are proof that 'inside the wretched hulk' there was a 'tiny spark' of goodness.[63] But for the Cunning Man, who represents the contagious poison of prejudice, there can be no forgiveness. Although Tiffany is able to 'feel the pain of a creature that had twisted through the world for hundreds of years',[64] and to wonder where evil begins, she lures him into the flaming stubble field where the hare ran into the fire and lets him burn.

All three of Pratchett's guardians – policeman, witch, and shepherd – live for their work, not out of worldly pride (although a little of that comes into it) but because it lies to their hand and urgently needs to be done. But being wedded to the job comes at a heavy price in human intimacy, though it is mitigated for Sam Vimes by his love for his formidable wife. 'Terrible is the temptation to do good!' Brecht says in *The Caucasian Chalk Circle*,[65] and Tiffany shares that temptation. When the kelda, the wise matriarch of the Nac Mac Feegle, questions her at the start of *The Shepherd's Crown* about her relationship with Preston, the young doctor who appears to be the perfect match for her, she replies, 'we like our work, both of us, in fact you might say we *are* our work [...] And I can't help thinking about Granny Aching and how much she liked her life, up on the downs ...'[66] At the end of the novel, when Tiffany has chosen to live in a shepherd's hut high up on the Chalk, she has a vision of 'two figures, both strangely familiar',[67] Granny Aching and Granny Weatherwax, side by side. Witches come in threes, and since her two dead but still omnipresent elders are the mother and the crone, it is Tiffany's role, at least for now, to be the maiden.

Working with his editor on *Snuff*, Pratchett was incensed to be told, 'You know usually in a career like yours, round about now would be the time that you would kill off a major character.'[68] When he actually does so in his final novel, the dedication page reads: 'For Esmerelda Weatherwax – mind how you go.'[69] It might seem a bleak and lonely death, meticulously prepared for in solitude, but Esme Weatherwax has the company of an old acquaintance, almost an old friend, who tells her, 'I CAN SEE THE BALANCE AND YOU HAVE LEFT THE WORLD MUCH BETTER THAN YOU FOUND IT.'[70] The Death of Discworld is 'implacable, because that is his job', but unlike Death in Bergman's *Seventh Seal*, he is 'a kindly Death, cleaning up the mess that this life leaves, and opening the gate to the next one. Indeed, in some religions he is an angel.'[71] He is also no chess-player. Only able to think in straight lines, 'he always forgets how the knights move'.[72]

In Paul Kidby's painting, *Check Mort*, Sir Terry in his trademark hat sits opposite his most popular character, smiling cheerfully, as a skeletal hand hovers over the chess board between them. Kidby has arranged the pieces to ensure that the Knight will win the game.[73]

. . . .

Judith Woolf

Notes

1.   Terry Pratchett, 'Imaginary Worlds: Real Stories', *Folklore* 111 (2000), 160.
2.   Terry Pratchett, *A Slip of the Keyboard: Collected Non-Fiction* (London: Corgi, 2015), 335.
3.   *Terry Pratchett HisWorld: Official Exhibition Companion* (London: Dunmanifestin Ltd, 2018), 184.
4.   Terry Pratchett and Paul Kidby, *The Art of Discworld* (London: Gollancz, 2005), no page number.
5.   Ingmar Bergman, *Det sjunde inseglet* (*The Seventh Seal*) (Göteborg: Rock! Editions, 1957), 13.
6.   Tristram Fane Saunders, 'Meticulously crafted, HisWorld shows why Terry Pratchett was his generation's Dickens', *The Telegraph*, 16 September 2017.
7.   A.S. Byatt, 'A comforting way of death', *The Guardian*, 9 November 2002.
8.   A.S. Byatt, 'Harry Potter and the Childish Adult', *The New York Times*, 7 July 2003.
9.   A.S. Byatt, 'A comforting way of death'.
10. Terry Pratchett and Jacqueline Simpson, *The Folklore of Discworld* (London: Corgi, 2009), 10.
11. Terry Pratchett, *Reaper Man* (London: Corgi, 1992), 7.
12. Jonathan Jones, 'I've read Pratchett now: it's more entertainment than art', *The Guardian*, 11 September 2015.
13. Terry Pratchett and Mark Lawson, *The Big Question*, BBC Television, 1 February 1998.
14. Terry Pratchett, *Carpe Jugulum* (London: Corgi, 1993), 370.
15. Susan Warner, 'Jesus bids us shine', *The Scottish Psalter and Church Hymnary* (Oxford University Press, 1929), 812.
16. Matthew, 5:16, King James Version.
17. Pratchett, *Carpe Jugulum*, 278.
18. Bergman, *Det sjunde inseglet*, 12.
19. Pratchett, *Carpe Jugulum*, 231.
20. *Ibid.*
21. Pratchett, *A Slip of the Keyboard*, 260.
22. Pratchett, *A Slip of the Keyboard*, 355.
23. Terry Pratchett, *Small Gods* (London: Corgi, 1993), 118.
24. Terry Pratchett, *Lords and Ladies* (London: Corgi, 1993), 342.
25. Terry Pratchett, *Maskerade* (London: Corgi, 1996), 98.
26. Pratchett, *Carpe Jugulum*, 349.
27. Pratchett, *Carpe Jugulum*, 350.
28. Pratchett, *Carpe Jugulum*, 420.
29. Pratchett, *Carpe Jugulum*, 421.
30. Pratchett and Lawson, *The Big Question*.
31. Rupert Goodwin, 'Magical Mayhem', *The Times*, 5 March 1994.
32. Jane Austen, *Northanger Abbey* (1818), chapter XXXI.
33. Pratchett, *Carpe Jugulum*, 50.
34. Terry Pratchett, *Mort* (London: Corgi, 1988), 84.
35. Pratchett and Lawson, *The Big Question*.
36. Pratchett, *Small Gods*, 100.

37. Terry Pratchett, 'Words from the Master', *The L-Space Web* (2002), https://www.lspace.org/books/apf/words-from-the-master.html (accessed 28 March 2021).
38. Pratchett, *Small Gods*, 380.
39. Pratchett, *Small Gods*, 100.
40. Pratchett, *Small Gods*, 101.
41. Pratchett, *Small Gods*, 207.
42. Terry Pratchett, *A Hat Full of Sky* (London: Corgi, 2005), 306.
43. Pratchett, *A Hat Full of Sky*, 309.
44. Pratchett, *A Hat Full of Sky*, 313.
45. Terry Pratchett, *The Shepherd's Crown* (London: Doubleday: 2015), 36.
46. Pratchett, *A Slip of the Keyboard*, 348.
47. Pratchett, *A Slip of the Keyboard*, 337.
48. Terry Pratchett, *I Shall Wear Midnight* (London: Doubleday, 2010), 81.
49. Pratchett, *A Slip of the Keyboard*, 312.
50. Terry Pratchett, *Wintersmith* (London: Corgi, 2007), 174.
51. Terry Pratchett, *The Wee Free Men* (London: Corgi, 2004), 151.
52. Pratchett, *The Wee Free Men*, 148.
53. Pratchett, *I Shall Wear Midnight*, 189-90.
54. Ginny Dougary, 'Terry Pratchett on the right to choose a good death', *Radio Times*, June 2011.
55. Pratchett, *I Shall Wear Midnight*, 294.
56. Pratchett, *A Hat Full of Sky*, 191.
57. Terry Pratchett, *Snuff* (London: Doubleday, 2011), 116.
58. Pratchett, *Carpe Jugulum*, 312.
59. Pratchett, *A Hat Full of Sky*, 250.
60. Pratchett and Lawson, *The Big Question*.
61. Pratchett, *The Wee Free Men*, 196.
62. Pratchett, *I Shall Wear Midnight*, 59.
63. *Ibid.*
64. Pratchett, *I Shall Wear Midnight*, 320.
65. Bertolt Brecht, *The Caucasian Chalk Circle*, trans. James and Tania Stern with W.H. Auden (London: Methuen, 1963), 25.
66. Pratchett, *The Shepherd's Crown*, 13.
67. Pratchett, *The Shepherd's Crown*, 331.
68. 'Terry Pratchett Interviewed', *Writers Online*, accessed 28 March 2021, https://www.writers-online.co.uk/how-to-write/creative-writing/terry-pratchett-interviewed/.
69. Pratchett, *The Shepherd's Crown*, iii.
70. Pratchett, *The Shepherd's Crown*, 38.
71. Pratchett, *A Slip of the Keyboard*, 335-6.
72. Pratchett and Kidby, *The Art of Discworld*, no page number.
73. *Terry Pratchett HisWorld*, 170.

Fig. I Gustave Doré's engraving, 'She Was Astonished
To See How Her Grandmother Looked' (1862),
an illustration of Perrault's 'Le Petit Chaperon Rouge'.

24

Little Red Riding Hood: A Discourse of Disciplinary Punishment

Claudia R. Barnett

Historically, the scholarship and social discourse attached to the Little Red Riding Hood fairy tale have held the protagonist accountable for her own violation and murder.[1] In part, this is due to the moral framing of her story and how her behaviour has been interpreted. Through this process and various retellings, the character and her crimson cloak have become iconic symbols of agentic female sexuality. John Stephens and Robyn McCallum argue that retold stories, 'especially folk and fairy tale … initiate children into aspects of social heritage, transmitting many of a culture's central values and assumptions'.[2] These traditional narratives, constructed from interlocking ideological frameworks, reveal the 'existential concerns of a society' through 'concrete images and symbolic forms … offering a cultural inheritance subject to social conditioning and modification through the interaction of various retellings'.[3] In recent times, a more sympathetic portrayal of Little Red Riding Hood as a victim of the wolf has emerged in western society.[4] These shifts reflect a changing perception towards violence against women.

Little Red Riding Hood made her literary debut in 1695 in a collection of fairy tales written by Charles Perrault. This manuscript was given (and dedicated) to Louis XIV's 19-year-old unmarried niece, Élisabeth Charlotte d'Orléans.[5] Perrault's story depicts a maiden's implicit rape and murder by a sexual predator. Superficially, it is a cautionary tale which advocates female celibacy before marriage. A closer inspection highlights the use of disciplinary punishment to silence the voices of the girl and her grandmother. The mother is mostly silent too. After uttering two sentences in the opening paragraph, she is absent from the story. Traditional retellings based on Perrault's work encode violence against women, social etiquette, gender roles and responsibilities, and hegemonic adult/child, male/female power structures. These practices and the structuring of silent femininity suggests these themes had social value in the cultures which generated the narratives.

Louis XIV's reign was a hedonistic era, overshadowed by public displays of disciplinary punishment. Michel Foucault's research on the 17th-century French penal system is a useful tool for examining the ideological frameworks constructed in Perrault's narrative, and other versions of Little Red Riding Hood; the most notable being the Grimms' 'Little Red Cap' (1812)[6] and Paul Delarue's 'The Story of Grandmother' (1951).[7] All three narratives contain similar themes of female sexuality and punishment, which have attracted the attention of academics.

Foucault theorises that forms of disciplinary punishment, such as public torture and execution, encouraged witnesses to conform to the law. Foucault argues that 'power produces knowledge',[8] and that power-knowledge discourse is formed by governing bodies and people with knowledge of the law and medicine.[9] These narratives identify and inhibit unacceptable social behaviour and are reinforced through hegemonic institutions such as parliament, schools, churches and penal systems. People are socialised to accept these discourses as the norm and use them as moral guides.

Seventeenth-century French fairy tales were originally written to entertain adults: Louis XIV's courtiers, members of the Académie française,[10] and those who attended the Parisian fairy tale salons. The latter were hosted at the homes of female fairy tale writers, the conteuses, who gave voice to their political views through their stories.[11] Their texts featured agentic and powerful female protagonists: characters who expressed concerns over arranged marriages and a woman's lack of autonomy within the gender hierarchy. Over time and through various retellings, this subversive mode of discourse evolved to transmit hegemonic ideologies and indoctrinate children.

Scholarly impressions of the Little Red Riding Hood fairy tales are varied. Academics such as Bruno Bettelheim,[12] Paul Delarue,[13] Yvonne Verdier,[14] Alan Dundes,[15] Jack Zipes,[16] Catherine Orenstein[17] and Marina Warner,[18] among others, have researched the literary and folkloric history of the tale. Collectively, this body of work has substantially added to contemporary understanding of how the narrative has evolved over the centuries, through different cultures and various adaptations. The themes of seduction, implied rape and female sexuality as constructed in Perrault's narrative (and in later retellings by the Grimms and Delarue) have also drawn much academic attention. Bettelheim questions the character's innocence leading up to the implied rape and argues that she is complicit in her own demise. Orenstein disagrees with Bettelheim's psychoanalytical approach, yet even she concedes that while Perrault's 17th-century 'stranger-danger' moral survives, 'in popular culture sweet Little Red Riding Hood has grown up and become an ode to Lust'.[19]

These observations illuminate how social discourse can shape a literary character's identity. The question then arises: is the evolving pop culture discourse in turn influenced by academic scholarship? Zipes has been described as one of the most prolific critics of literary fairy tales,[20] while Bettelheim's work has been described as 'the best-known psychoanalytic interpretation of the Little Red Riding Hood narrative'.[21] David Fisher, Bettelheim's biographer, states he:

> operated as a public intellectual whose writings and pronouncements were eagerly awaited, widely disseminated, and published in distinguished large circulation magazines and journals ... his ideas and opinions had a huge impact on a large reading audience ...[22]

By creating a dialogue with a fairy tale which promotes female chastity, Bettelheim's text encouraged readers to adhere to conservative gender behaviour. His work is a good example of how a person in a position of 'power' can produce knowledge through discourse. Some of Bettelheim's theories are now disputed but his analyses contribute towards fairy tale interpretations within academic circles and pop culture discourse.[23] Consequently, his body of work continues to have a voice in the dialogue related to this fairy-tale heroine.

The Uses of Enchantment, Bettelheim's Freudian analysis of popular fairy tales, was published in America in 1976. His study of the Little Red Riding Hood narratives endorsed conservative, patriarchal views on female sexuality during the western sexual revolution. Bettelheim introduces Little Red Riding Hood to his audience as a 'charming, "innocent" young girl swallowed by a Wolf'.[24] His use of inverted commas for the word 'innocent' positions readers to question the morality of the character before he even begins his discussion. He then uses Lang's English translation (1889)[25] to deconstruct Perrault's story after the heroine arrives at Grandmother's house.[26]

In Lang's translation, the meeting between wolf and child unfolds in the following manner:

> Little Red Riding-Hood pulled the bobbin, and the door opened.
> The Wolf, seeing her come in, said to her, hiding himself under the
> bed-clothes:
>
> "Put the custard and the little pot of butter upon the stool, and
> come and lie down with me."
>
> Little Red Riding-Hood undressed herself and went into bed,
> where, being greatly amazed to see how her grandmother looked
> in her night-clothes, she said to her ...[27]

Little Red Riding Hood, unable to perceive the threat presented by the wolf, trustingly obeys her pseudo-grandmother. And Lang, who was writing for children, specifically notes that Grandmother was wearing 'her night-clothes'.

Bettelheim altered Lang's text to support his theory that Perrault's character was a 'fallen woman'. He omits the description of the wolf concealing his identity. He writes:

> In Perrault's story the wolf does not dress up as Grandmother, but
> simply lies down in her bed. When Little Red Riding Hood
> arrived, the wolf asked her to join him in bed. Little Red Riding
> Hood undressed and got into bed, at which moment, astonished at
> how Grandmother looked naked ...[28]

Bettelheim's version positions readers to think that when the child entered the house, she immediately saw the animal undisguised, and willingly joined him in bed. His textual modification also supports his theory that the heroine was sexually promiscuous. He argues:

> when the wolf tells her that his strong arms are for embracing her better nothing is left to the imagination. Since in response to such direct and obvious seduction Little Red Riding Hood makes no move to escape or fight back, either she is stupid or wants to be seduced ... Little Red Riding Hood is changed from a naive, attractive young girl ... into nothing but a fallen woman.[29]

Bettelheim also identifies the Grimms' heroine, Rotkappchen, as a pubescent girl with a 'pleasure-seeking id' whose premature, 'budding' sexuality is a danger to herself and others.[30] Bettelheim argues that Rotkappchen battles her unacknowledged Oedipal desire to seduce her father, symbolically represented by both the wolf and huntsman,[31] and arranges 'things so that the wolf can do away with the mother figure', i.e. Grandmother: her aging rival for the wolf's attention.[32] This occurs when Rotkappchen willingly gives the wolf directions to Grandmother's house.[33] The removal of this authority figure frees the child to act on her subconscious desire to seduce and be seduced.[34] This enables her to explore her sexuality with the father/wolf/hunter figure.

Bettelheim maintains that the grandmother contributed to the child's unruly behaviour because she spoils her granddaughter and 'abdicates her own attractiveness to males and transfers it to the daughter by giving her a too attractive red cloak'.[35] His use of the words 'too attractive' in relation to the red cloak suggests Grandmother dressed her female child in a sexually provocative outfit, one which encourages negative male attention. The character's name is linked to the colour red, 'which she openly wears, a colour that signifies 'violent, sexual emotions'.[36] Through his analysis, Rotkappchen flouts her sexuality and readers are positioned to view the character, and agentic female sexuality, as inherently sensual and sinful.

During her analysis of the red hood/cape in Perrault's text, Orenstein creates a similar interpretation. She writes: 'Perrault cloaked his heroine in red, the colour of harlots, scandal and blood, symbolizing her sin and foreshadowing her fate'.[37] She argues that Perrault's moral pre-text warns of the 'dangers of female promiscuity'.[38] Zipes also observes that in 17th-century France, the colour red was associated with 'sin, sensuality and the devil'.[39] He argues that the red hood, a gift from her indulgent grandmother, was a warning to the implied female reader that the heroine could be 'spoiled in another way by a wolf/man'.[40] Through Zipes' lens, the 'spoiled' child was accustomed to being at the centre of attention. When she stopped to talk to the wolf, she created her own downfall.

The red hood/cap is missing in Delarue's narrative. However, in the Grimms' and Perrault's versions, this article of clothing is so important both the narrative and character are identified by it. Perrault's text was written in an age and culture when aristocratic families secured important social alliances through arranged marriages.[41] Orenstein notes that a 1629 ordinance declared that paternal consent was legally required for all French marriages, regardless of the offspring's age. Failure to comply was punishable by death.[42]

The bride's virginity ensured that any child born after the union was a legitimate heir to their combined fortunes.[43] To help ensure their purity until they came of age, aristocratic daughters were usually cloistered within a convent from as young as four years of age until they were married.[44] During her discussion on 17th-century regional French bridal attire, Gibson records that on their wedding day, the 'peasant bride of Touraine favoured colour and sparkle with her scarlet robe and head-dress embroidered with imitation jewellery'.[45] It was likely Perrault was familiar with this custom as his mother came from Touraine.[46] From this socio-historical perspective, the red hood does not align the character with sin, sensuality and the devil. Rather, it references 17th-century French marriage customs and highlights the implicit theme of marriage interwoven within the tale. When the heroine disrobes and enters the bed at the wolf/grandmother's command, she was unknowingly rejecting the respectability of the marriage bed. The finality of her 'death' symbolically represents her future exile from respectable/'polite' social circles. It also reinforces the *moralité* of the story and reveals a societal concern for young girls to comply with hegemonic cultural discourse relating to arranged marriages.

However, another reading can be drawn from the text and the significance of the red hood/cloak in 17th-century France. In this reading, Perrault's, the Grimms' and Delarue's heroine is an innocent victim/ prey. In part, her death occurs due to the structuring of social etiquette and the promotion of childhood obedience to adult authority figures. In Perrault's text, the wolf is portrayed as an 'old neighbour' wolf /man.[47] The word 'neighbour' and the character's friendly response implies he and the heroine are known to each other (at least in passing). This explains why she stopped to talk to him – she is not encouraging his sexual advances; she is merely being polite.

The power structures created by the text privileges the adult male in the adult/child, male/female relationship. The protagonist (and, through her experiences, the reader) learns that she is powerless in her social encounter with the adult, male wolf-man. When Little Red Riding Hood immediately obeys the wolf/grandmother's command to undress and enter the bed, her behaviour demonstrates that childhood obedience was an important social construct in Perrault's time. And when the narrator informs the reader that 'the poor child … did not know that it is dangerous to stop and listen to the wolf',[48] this indicates that children were viewed as naive and ignorant in 17th-century constructions of childhood. This wording also portrays her as an innocent victim of the wolf and implicitly condemns the mother for being negligent in her parental duty. Hence the 'stranger danger' warning commonly extracted from this narrative.

In the *moralité*, the omniscient narrator warns the implied reader that if a young girl stops to listen to the wolf, 'it is not so strange the wolf shall eat them'. This implicit criticism is the only time the text positions readers to think that the victim might be at fault for encouraging the wolf. However, the sentence must be read in context with the rest of the paragraph. The final lines of the *moralité* state: 'But alas for those *who do not know* that of all the wolves the docile ones are ... most dangerous' (my italics).[49] This last sentence again exonerates the victim of all responsibility and reinforces the impression that she was ignorant of societal dangers.

Social etiquette is more strongly structured in the Grimms' retelling when the mother actively coaches her daughter how to behave on the way to grandmother's house. When the wolf (portrayed as a talking animal) greets the child, 'Good Day, Little Red Cap', she politely responds with: 'Thank you kindly, wolf.'[50] The wolf has addressed her by name so it is unsurprising that the child stops and replies. In this version, the wolf is a stranger. His knowledge of the character's identity implies he has been stalking her.

A foreshadowing of her fate as a victim of rape, and the loss of her virginity, is created when he proceeds to ask her 'What are you carrying under your apron?'[51] It is important to note that in both the Perrault and Grimms narratives, the child disobeys the mother and listens to the wolf when *he tells her* which path she should take. Unlike Delarue's text, she is not given a choice in these pre-texts. This indicates that patriarchal voice held more authority than feminine voice in the cultures that generated the text (i.e. 17th-century France and 19th-century Germany).

Collectively, the arguments of Bettelheim, Zipes and Orenstein identify Little Red Riding Hood as being sexually promiscuous. However, through close narrative analysis, Perrault and the Grimms' Little Red Riding Hood character emerges as a well-loved (not spoiled) little girl. She is adored by her family and all who 'laid eyes upon her'.[52] At her mother's bidding she leaves the matriarchal domain and enters the external political sphere: the forest, inhabited by patriarchal representatives, i.e. the woodsmen and wolf. This cherished child, who has never been treated harshly, has the confidence to speak freely to the wolf/man and ask a series of incessant questions from the 'loving' adult authority figure, represented by the wolf/grandmother during their infamous dialogue. However, after leaving the sheltered, feminine world of her home, the patriarchal representative teaches her that it is politically incorrect for her to question the patriarchy or *any other* authority figure.

Through a Foucauldian lens, readers are positioned to view Little Red Riding Hood's questioning of the wolf as 'bad' behaviour because the act of speaking has negative repercussions: both Little Red Riding Hood and her grandmother are *permanently* silenced, cast out of hegemonic society by their violent demise. The matriarchal voice is further stifled through the structuring of the mostly absent (and therefore silent) mother. This narrative motif is significant given that motherhood was an important social construct in Perrault's time.[53]

Foucault argues that punishment of the prisoner's mind and body is 'a complex social function … a political tactic … It is always the body that is at issue … its forces, their utility and their docility, their distributions and their submissions'.[54] Annette Iggulden draws a link between silent femininity and political gender power-discourse when she writes:

> Historically, the speech and silence of women appears intricately intertwined with and shaped by attitudes borne from various visual and verbal discourses about their bodies … the naturalisation of silence and passivity as feminine virtues had left women profoundly vulnerable to the exercise of male power and control.[55]

Foucault's and Iggulden's theories can be applied effectively not only to 'Little Red Riding Hood', but other traditional western fairy tales such as 'Snow White', 'Cinderella' and 'Sleeping Beauty'. In these stories, the silence of women is a recurring theme closely associated with punishment and/or death of the female body. Perrault's Cinderella and Sleeping Beauty are rewarded for their silence and obedience with romantic love, advantageous marriages, wealth, and acceptance into the highest echelon of their society. Their marital reward promotes female passivity and silence as desirable feminine qualities which have been normalised and further endorsed through the reprinting and retelling of these familiar stories.[56] However Little Red Riding Hood, who is arguably one of the more vocal female protagonists, breaks the 'happily ever after' fairy-tale mould.

As mentioned earlier, in the late 17th century, aristocratic women hosted literary salons in their homes. Their conversation included debates concerning arranged marriages and protests against laws inhibiting women from owning property. Anti-feminist propaganda was generated in response to this type of feminist discourse and circulated freely in French society.[57] Warner writes that salon hostesses also held large gatherings in their bedchambers while lounging in bed. Favoured guests were allowed access to the '*ruelle*' which Warner defines as:

> the alley — which was the space between her bed and the wall. Ruelles became the word for such salons … those who attended were called alcôvistes, privy to the alcôve. This arrangement of social space, both public and private at the same time, was presided over by women …[58]

A reference to this feminine seat of power, and feminist discourse, is constructed in Perrault's text when the narrator informs the reader that the wolf follows 'young ladies right into their homes, right into their alcoves'.[59] In Perrault's and the Grimms' text, the grandmother is lying in bed when the wolf arrives. He tricks her into allowing him access to her home and kills her as she lies in bed, thus appropriating her matriarchal domain, her feminine seat of power (represented by the bed), her identity and her voice. By masquerading as grandmother he then uses all these authoritative feminine attributes to manipulate the girl-child in order to permanently silence *her*.

In the Grimms' retelling, both the wolf and the hunter appropriate feminine roles traditionally associated with feminine autonomy and power (i.e. motherhood and midwifery, respectively). This occurs when the wolf swallows the grandmother and child and a passing hunter rescues them by slicing open the wolf's abdomen and performing a laparotomy/pseudo-caesarean section. Zipes utilises Foucault's theories to argue that the Grimms' heroine demonstrates her repentance (for sexual transgressions) with a symbolic act of disciplinary punishment. He writes:

> The Grimms were responsible for making Little Red Riding Hood definitively into a disobedient, helpless little girl ... She is much more fully to blame for her rape by the wolf because she has a nonconformist streak which must be eradicated ... a policeman appears out of nowhere to save Little Red Riding Hood, and, when she is granted the opportunity to punish the wolf by filling his stomach with rocks, she is actually punishing herself ...[60]

In Zipes' scenario, the act of swallowing the child is a sexual act because when she is devoured she becomes a part of the wolf.[61] The hunter/policeman's disciplinary punishment teaches the child to 'internalize ... the restraining norms of sexuality'.[62] Granny, too, gains wisdom from her experience and both females combine forces to defeat a second wolf later in the narrative. This structuring demonstrates that both females were reborn at the hands of the male 'midwife' as patriarchal constructs of 'good' femininity. Within a Foucauldian framework, the act of retrieving stones as a symbolic form of disciplinary punishment is a reasonable assumption. However, a close reading of the text reveals the hegemonic gender power hierarchy: the female characters are powerless against the brute strength and authority of the male characters. Furthermore, the consumption of Little Red Riding Hood makes her a victim; she is not sexually complicit in her demise.

Zipes also examines Perrault's tale as a discourse of rape and violence against women, written by a male author.[63] Zipes writes: 'Perrault's historical contribution to the image of Little Red Riding Hood ... must be viewed in light of French social history and Perrault's own personal prejudices'.[64] In this manner, the story emerges as 'projection of male phantasy in a literary discourse ... aimed at curbing the natural inclinations of children'.[65] Zipes argues that the structuring of the child's discipline and punishment in Perrault's tale and various adaptations reveals social concerns and the regulation of sex roles and sexuality.[66] From Zipes' perspective,

Perrault 'contaminated'[67] a 17th-century oral tale (as recorded by Delarue in 1951),[68] and in doing so, he converted an innocent, plucky folklore heroine into an objectified sexual being.

Zipes observes that Little Red Riding Hood's reputation as a *femme fatale* has evolved from the themes of seduction, violence and rape woven into Perrault's literary classic.[69] His own interest in Little Red Riding Hood was piqued by exposure to pop culture images and social advertisements featuring her persona. He writes:

> What attracted me to Little Red Riding Hood in the first place was 'her' commodified appearance as a sex object, and how I was socialized to gaze at her gazing at me ...[70]

Zipes later examined the narratives in light of the rape culture discourse prevalent in western society. His discussion was written in the 1990s following a spree of sexual crimes committed against women by a serial rapist.[71] Zipes highlights societal concerns regarding female safety and gendered violence and observes that the hegemonic Western rape narrative blames female victims for their violation. This dialogue has seeped into popular discourse (books, films, cartoons etc.). Zipes cites Perrault's story as an example and argues that while the story presents a useful 'stranger danger' warning for girls, it also 'reinforces the notion that "women want to be raped"'.[72]

Foucault identifies sexuality as a 'dense transfer point for relations of power: between men and women, young people and old people, parents and offspring.'[73] Bettelheim's interpretation of the Doré print illustrates this theory ('She Was Astonished To See How Her Grandmother Looked', 1862, Fig. 1). The print depicts the infamous bed scene Bettelheim uses to construct his 'Fallen Woman' narrative. Bettelheim notes:

> She makes no move to leave. She seems ... attracted and repelled at the same time ... The combination of feelings her face and body suggest can best be described as fascination ... the same fascination which sex, and everything surrounding it, exercises over the child's mind ...[74]

Here Bettelheim argues that because the child *chose* to stay in bed with the wolf, her sexual agency and attraction to the wolf are to blame for her implicit rape and murder. This transforms the child victim into an empowered sexualised female. It also exemplifies Foucault's theory of how 'discourse can be both an instrument and an effect of power', but also a 'starting point for an opposing strategy'.[75]

Orenstein implicitly endorses Bettelheim's theory when she notes that Doré's print captures the couple in:

> an intimate cliché … it's as if we're peering through the keyhole
> into an old Parisian boudoir … The bed fills the picture frame …
> The girl's loosened hair tumbles over her shoulders; she clutches
> the sheets to her breast.[76]

Her evocative language portrays the heroine as an alluring female, a willing participant in her seduction and implicit rape. She writes that what 'Doré captured, and Bettelheim later enhanced', is the story's 'buried meaning as a sexual parable'.[77] Orenstein examines the story against the backdrop of Louis XIV's debauched court. She notes that the reference to the wolf in Perrault's text was significant from a socio-historical viewpoint. The term 'she'd seen the wolf' indicated a loss of virginity.[78] Orenstein explains that 'any courtier who read this tale' would have understood the meaning as it was part of the common slang.[79] This implies the term predated Perrault's text.

In his paper 'A Second Gaze at Little Red Riding Hood's Trials and Tribulations' (1983-4), Zipes makes similar observations during his analysis of Doré's print:

> Doré also suggests that it is primarily she who is asking for it.
> And, what is it? The erotic display … confirms what we suppose
> to be true about both women and men: women want men to
> rape them … men are … weak beasts … tempted by alluring
> female creatures.[80]

Zipes argues that the scene captures the couple engaged in prohibited extramarital behaviour. He writes:

> the longing if not seductive look of Little Red Riding Hood as she
> peers into the eyes of the wolf, and her faint smile … the
> proximity of wolf and girl who appear to be touching and to be
> totally absorbed in an intimate tête à tête … Doré stresses the
> desire of the girl and wolf for one another. But, by revealing the
> full face of the girl and her apparent seductive glance, Doré also
> suggests it is primarily she who is asking for it. And, what is it?
> In this case it is an immense wolf or phallus …[81]

Through this interpretation, Little Red Riding Hood is again transformed into a seductive female who actively encourages the wolf's advances. Zipes notes that Perrault's heroine is 'too stupid'[82] to outwit the wolf or discern the type of danger he represents. Here, Zipes is comparing Perrault's character with Delarue's, who outwits the wolf and escapes. Zipes argues that Perrault's heroine is 'spoiled, negligent and naïve'.[83] Her red chaperon transforms her into 'a type of bourgeois girl tainted with sin, since red, like the scarlet letter A, recalls the devil and heresy'.[84] Zipes' discussion on the western rape narrative draws attention to how it can emerge in social discourse. He also creates awareness of how cultural norms are formed through society's repeated exposure to narrative threads.

In scholarship attached to her story, Little Red Riding Hood has been called stupid, a fallen woman, a femme fatale, and other derogatory terms. Some argue that she is complicit in her own rape and demise, and responsible for her grandmother's death.[85] This reinforces negative stereotypes of femininity in relation to her character. She has been linked to the western rape culture through academic and pop culture discourse. As such, we need to consider the effect academic power discourse may have upon the victim-blaming rape narrative and how this, in turn, can disempower women who have been sexually assaulted.

In light of this, I would like to offer an alternative deconstruction of Doré's illustration. Here is a child in a defensive rather than seductive pose. Her right arm and shoulder are protectively raised. The downward tilt of her head emphasises her guarded response to the wolf. Furthermore, the corner of her lips are compressed and she is frowning. Admittedly, she does not look afraid while conversing with the wolf; however, the widened eyes indicate wariness. The wolf is invading her personal space and overshadowing her as he leans in towards her and gazes directly at her body. The downward tilt of his eyebrows and his unsmiling mouth appear unfriendly and threatening. In response, the child's torso is tilted backwards, away from the wolf. She holds the sheet up protectively between them so that it completely covers the right side of her body (including her arm), which is closest to the wolf, and she rests the material against the lower part of her face. Her left hand crosses over her chest in a defensive manner and anchors the sheet in position. Even her knees (beneath the blanket) are turned away from the wolf, as though she will leap out of the bed at any moment. Collectively, these observations paint her as the wolf's victim, rather than a willing participant.

Foucault argues that '[d]iscourse transmits and produces power; it reinforces it, but also undermines and exposes it, renders it fragile and makes it possible to thwart it'.[86] In recent years, there has been a slight shift in how women who have experienced gendered violence are perceived. Little Red Riding Hood's social image has changed too. For those familiar with her story, her iconic red cloak can be linked to social injustice and accountability. An example of this is the red headgear worn by Steve McCurry's 'Afghan Girl' (1984) and Jack Lack's street art portrayal of the same image entitled 'Steve McCurry's Girl' (Fig. 2).

McCurry's portrait of Sharbat Gula appeared on the 1985 cover of *National Geographic*. An accompanying caption proclaimed the child's 'haunted eyes tell of an Afghan refugee's fears'.[87] Gula's constricted pupils and dishevelled dark hair amplify her wary expression and her features are framed by a red burka. This unique combination and the subject's age creates an inadvertent intertextual reference to Little Red Riding Hood. This implicitly links the literary character

Fig. 2 Jack Lack's street art illustration 'Steve McCurry's Girl' was inspired by Steve McCurry's 'Afghan Girl'.
Artwork and photograph of artwork: Jack Lack. Instagram: @jack_lack_
Original photo/source material: Steve McCurry. Instagram: @stevemccurryofficial

(a victim of patriarchal power) to the subjugated female refugees of a patriarchal political war.

In Lack's interpretation of McCurry's work, the girl's blurred, fragmented image and solemn features highlight the original subject's difficult experiences as an Afghan refugee. Lack also transformed the rusty colour of the original burka to a deep crimson. The draped material resembles a hooded cloak which further heightens her resemblance to Little Red Riding Hood.

The red clothing worn by Lack's and McCurry's girls connects female victims of social injustice to the Little Red Riding Hood character. Yet her story has always been linked to gendered violence against women and this continues in pop culture narratives. An example of this is Eddie White's cartoon (2018, Fig. 3), which circulated on Australian Facebook pages (including the Australian Fairy Tale Society's) after the 2018 rape and murder of Eurydice Dixon.[88] This Melbournian woman was stalked in a park after dark by a sexual predator. It was the fourth similar (but unrelated) incident to occur in Melbourne within a 12-month period. Eurydice's name was never attached to the image in the Facebook posts, but the timing of the posts and the nature of the crimes committed against her created an unspoken connection between this innocent young

She dreamt of a world where she safely walked wherever she wished. Whenever she pleased. Wearing whatever she liked. For the village protected her from the wolves.

Fig. 3 Eddie White's Little Red Riding Hood illustration (2018) circulated on Australian Facebook pages following the rape and murder of Eurydice Dixon.

victim and the illustration of Little Red Riding Hood. White's image demands social accountability and change in relation to sex crimes against women. It also challenges preconceived notions of Little Red Riding Hood being held responsible for her violation and murder.

Delarue's wolf first encounters the heroine at the crossroads while she is journeying to Grandmother's house and he asks her to choose between the path of pins or needles. French ethnographer Yvonne Verdier interprets the tale through her knowledge of 19th-century French peasant culture whereby girls at the age of 15 undertook apprenticeships as seamstresses. Verdier argues that from within this ethnographic context the child must decide whether to stay an adolescent (represented by the pins), or move forwards into womanhood (represented by the needles).[89] Zipes and Verdier argue that Delarue's text presents a hopeful tale of female maturation.[90] This is because Delarue's protagonist uniquely outwits the wolf and makes her escape.[91] When comparing Perrault's pre-text to Delarue's version, Zipes writes that Perrault 'transformed a hopeful oral tale … into a tragic one of violence in which the girl is blamed for her own violation', whereas Delarue 'celebrates the self-reliance of a young peasant girl'.[92]

However, Delarue's discourse explicitly structures the heroine as a sexual tease and 'salope' (slut).[93] Delarue writes: 'After she had eaten, there was a little cat which said: "Phooey! … A slut is she who eats the flesh and drinks the blood of her granny."'[94] Unlike Perrault's asexual character (who undresses in a matter-of-fact manner before entering the bed), Delarue's heroine enacts an elaborate striptease for the wolf as he lounges in Granny's bed:

> "Where should I put my apron?"
> "Throw it into the fire, my child, you won't be needing it anymore."
> And each time she asked where she should put all her other clothes, the bodice, the dress, the petticoat, and the long stockings, the wolf responded …[95]

A Foucauldian analysis reveals a deeper, underlying thread of disciplinary punishment and torture. The wolf's role as executioner is foreshadowed when he meets the heroine 'à la croisée' (at the crossroads).[96] In his study of the 17th-century French penal system, Foucault explains that the corpses of condemned prisoners were exhibited 'at one of the near-by crossroads'. These corpses served as a deterrent against crime for all those who passed by.[97] The public executioner (like the wolf) lived outside the parameters of hegemonic society and wore a mask as part of his persona. In traditional Little Red Riding

Hood narratives (including Delarue's), the wolf as executioner *masks* his identity when he dons Granny's clothes. Foucault refers to the practice of desecrating the body of the prisoner after death as another form of punishment and argues that the punishment of the prisoner took the 'form of humiliation and pain'.[98] This is demonstrated in Delarue's text when the wolf/executioner butchers granny's body into sections and drains the blood into a vessel before storing these items in the pantry. After Little Red Riding Hood arrives at the cottage, the wolf tortures his next victim when he tells her to 'eat the meat that's in the pantry and drink a bottle of wine that is on the shelf'.[99] After watching her cannibalise her grandmother, the wolf orders her to undress in front of him and join him in bed. In Delarue's text, the omniscient narrator and reading audience are privileged with knowledge of the wolf-grandmother's true identity. Like witnesses at a public execution, they observe the grandmother's and child's torture and granny's execution. The wolf's patriarchal control over the child is consistently demonstrated through his manipulation of the child and her obedience to his demands. This highlights the adult/child, male/female power hierarchy constructed within the text. Delarue's heroine, like her predecessors before her, is a victim of the predatory wolf.

However, unlike the maiden in Perrault's and the Grimms' version, Delarue's heroine outwits the wolf and saves herself, thereby inverting the power structure of the existing binaries. Delarue's text structures this power inversion through the child's feminine speech. This occurs when the child interrogates the wolf about his appearance as follows: "Oh, Granny, how hairy you are!"[100] As the dialogue progresses, readers become aware that the child has a growing awareness of Granny's true identity. She utilises the wolf's own deception (his pretence of being a doting grandmother and genteel woman) to manipulate the wolf into allowing her to go outside and relieve herself. He reluctantly agrees and ties a rope around her leg before allowing her to go outside. However, once she has left the house, she re-ties the rope to a tree and successfully escapes, thereby inverting the adult/child, powerful/powerless, knowledgeable/ignorant binaries the text has created between the male/female characters. A female folk hero is born.

This textual structuring illustrates Foucault's theory on temporary power inversion. Foucault explains that on the scaffold, condemned prisoners were allowed to say anything they wanted. In this manner, 'rules were inverted, authority mocked and criminals transformed into heroes'.[101] Foucault argues that it is possible for subjugated individuals to temporarily invert the power structure through their knowledge and understanding of power processes, and their struggles to navigate these power hierarchies.[102] Delarue's text positions readers to view the heroine as adaptable and courageous. She is no longer a victim of the predatory wolf. Yet there is no denying that her freedom came after she was subjected to acts of disciplinary punishment.

Little Red Riding Hood's evolving narrative is encoded with cultural gender values and power structures. Historically, these themes have been used to construct and reinforce victim blaming narratives in relation to this character. However, a socio-historical, Foucauldian reading of the original text revealed that the wolf is responsible for his own sexual crimes. He manipulated, deceived and silenced his female victims. A similar interpretation of the wolf's role is also possible for the Grimms' and Delarue's narratives. These readings challenge hegemonic academic and pop culture discourse related to this fairy-tale heroine.

In today's society, victims of sex crimes are still being silenced by shame, fear of repercussions and even murder. In relation to this, Foucault's theories on how power-discourse is formed and how it can be used to create social norms and inhibit unsavoury behaviour prove useful. Foucauldian theory, along with Zipes' analysis of western rape culture, illustrate how literary characters, while fictional, can still play a role in creating and reinforcing gender norms. This discussion questions the relationship between pop-culture discourse and scholarship and how each informs the other.

An examination of the varied academic approaches used to analyse Little Red Riding Hood's narratives indicates its relevance across many fields of scholarship, including pop culture discourse. It's clear that the story remains open to interpretation, but the terms used to describe literary victims of sexual abuse, particularly children, in those interpretations may have wider cultural implications. Perhaps, over time, with a more empathetic approach to the scholarship, academic power-discourse can play a role in altering the hegemonic western rape-culture narrative. This can change how real-life victims perceive themselves and encourage them to use their voice to obtain justice. It can also transform how we, as a society, see them. We need to create a compassionate, nurturing community where victims are encouraged to share their story.

. . . .

Claudia R. Barnett

Notes

1. Bruno Bettelheim argues that Little Red Riding Hood is 'stupid or she wants to be seduced' because she does not try to escape or fight the wolf's advances after she enters the bed (Bruno Bettelheim, *The Uses Of Enchantment: The Meaning and Importance of Fairy Tales*, 3rd edn (London: Penguin Books, 1991), 169). Furthermore, Jack Zipes describes Perrault's heroine as 'the helpless girl, who subconsciously contributed to her own rape' (Jack Zipes, *The Trials and Tribulations of Little Red Riding Hood*, 2nd edn (New York: Routledge, 1993), 27). Zipes offers a similar assessment of the Grimms' Little Red Cap when he explains that the character was punished for her 'disobedience and indulgence in sensual pleasures ... the wolf is sent to teach her and the audience a lesson. Her degradation and punishment set an example.' (Zipes, *Trials and Tribulations*, 33.) And, during her analyses of the fairy tale, Maria Tatar examines a 'verse melodrama' written by F.W.N. Bailey in 1862 (in Zipes, *Trials & Tribulations*, 158). Tartar explains the text 'made Little Red Riding Hood responsible for her own death and for her grandmother's demise' (Maria Tatar, *The Classic Fairy Tales: Texts, Criticism* (New York: W.W. Norton Company, 1999), 6).
2. John Stephens and Robin McCallum, *Retelling Stories, Framing Culture: Traditional Story and Metanarratives in Children's Literature* (New York & London: Garland Publishing, 1998), 4.
3. *Ibid.*
4. Susan Brownmiller identifies the Little Red Riding Hood story as a 'parable of rape' (Susan Brownmiller, *Against Our Will: Men, Women and Rape*, 4th edn (New York: Open Road Integrated Media, 2013), 343-4). Brownmiller examines the narrative as part of her discussion on patriarchal myths used to justify rape crimes. Brownmiller argues that both the child and her grandmother 'are equally defenceless before the male wolf's strength and cunning' (*Ibid.*). Eddie White's illustration, 'Little Red Riding Hood' (Fig. 3), also challenges hegemonic victim-blaming narratives and reminds his audience that society as a whole has a responsibility to keep potential victims safe from sexual predators. White's illustration is examined further in this paper.
5. Charles Perrault, *Contes De Mère l'Oyé* (France, 1695).
6. Jacob and Wilhelm Grimm, 'Little Red Cap (1812)', trans. Jack Zipes in Jack Zipes, *The Trials and Tribulations of Little Red Riding Hood*, ed. Jack Zipes, 2nd edn (New York: Routledge, 1993), 135-9.
7. Paul Delarue, 'Les Contes merveilleux de Perrault et la tradition populaire', *Bulletin folklorique d'Ile-de-France*, vol. 13 (1951): 221-8.
8. Michel Foucault, *Discipline and Punish: The Birth of the Prison*, trans. Alan Sheridan (New York: Vintage Books, 1979), 27.
9. Foucault, *Discipline and Punish*, 11 and 102.
10. Christina A. Jones, *Mother Goose Refigured: A Critical Translation of Charles Perrault's Fairy Tales* (Michigan: Wayne State University Press, 2016), 53.
11. Elizabeth Wanning Harries, *Twice Upon A Time: Women Writers and the History of the Fairy Tale* (New Jersey: Princeton University Press, 2001), 17.
12. Bruno Bettelheim, *The Uses Of Enchantment: The Meaning And Importance Of Fairy Tales*, 3rd edn (London: Penguin Books, 1991).
13. Delarue, Les Contes merveilleux de Perrault'.
14. Yvonne Verdier, 'Little Red Riding Hood in Oral Tradition', *Marvels & Tales*, vol. 11, no. 1/2 (1997): 101-23.
15. Alan Dundes, 'Introduction', in *Little Red Riding Hood: A Casebook*, ed. Alan Dundes (USA: The University of Wisconsin Press, 1989), ix-xi.
16. Jack Zipes, *The Trials and Tribulations of Little Red Riding Hood*, ed. Jack Zipes, 2nd edn (New York: Routledge, 1993).
17. Catherine Orenstein, *Little Red Riding Hood Uncloaked: Sex, Morality and the Evolution of a Fairy Tale* (New York: Basic Books, 2002).
18. Marina Warner, *From the Beast to the Blonde: On Fairy Tales and Their Tellers*, 2nd edn (London: Vintage, 1995).

19. Orenstein, *Little Red Riding Hood Uncloaked*, 6.
20. Jan Ziolkowski, 'A Fairy Tale from before Fairy Tales: Egbert of Liege's "De puella a lupellis seruata" and the Medieval Background of "Little Red Riding Hood"', *Speculum: A Journal of Medieval Studies* (1992), vol. 67, no. 3/Jul.: 551.
21. Dundes, 'Introduction', *Little Red Riding Hood: A Casebook*, 217.
22. David J. Fisher, *Bettelheim: Living and Dying* (Rodopi, 2008), 1.
23. Dundes, *Little Red Riding Hood: A Casebook*, 220; Warner, *From the Beast to the Blonde*, 213; Orenstein, *Little Red Riding Hood Uncloaked*, 193; Peter Arnds, 'Absent Mother and the Wolf in Little Red Riding Hood', *Neophilologus* (2017), vol. 101: 175-85; Marcia K Lieberman, '"Some Day My Prince Will Come"; female acculturation through the fairy tale', in Jack Zipes (ed.), *Don't Bet On The Prince: Contemporary Feminist Fairy Tales in North America and England* (Gower Publishing, 1986), 187.
24. Bettelheim, *The Uses of Enchantment*, 166.
25. Andrew Lang, *The Blue Fairy Book* (1989), Sacred Texts, http://www.sacred-texts.com/neu/lfb/bl/ (accessed 16 July 2017).
26. Bettelheim, *The Uses of Enchantment*, 167-8.
27. Lang, *The Blue Fairy Book*.
28. Bettelheim, *The Uses of Enchantment*, 167.
29. Bettelheim, *The Uses of Enchantment*, 167-8.
30. Bettelheim, *The Uses of Enchantment*, 173.
31. Bettelheim, *The Uses of Enchantment*, 175.
32. Bettelheim, *The Uses of Enchantment*, 172.
33. Bettelheim, *The Uses of Enchantment*, 173.
34. Bettelheim, *The Uses of Enchantment*, 175.
35. Bettelheim, *The Uses of Enchantment*, 173.
36. *Ibid.*
37. Orenstein, *Little Red Riding Hood Uncloaked*, 36.
38. *Ibid.*
39. Zipes, *Trials and Tribulations*, 26.
40. *Ibid.*
41. Wendy Gibson, *Women In Seventeenth-Century France* (London: Macmillan Press, 1989), 58.
42. Orenstein, *Little Red Riding Hood Uncloaked*, 36.
43. Gibson, *Women In Seventeenth-Century France*, 63.
44. Orenstein, *Little Red Riding Hood Uncloaked*, 36.
45. Gibson, *Women In Seventeenth-Century France*, 63.
46. Zipes notes that Perrault's mother grew up in Touraine and would have heard of the 1598 werewolf trial which took place there. Thus, Perrault would have been familiar with oral werewolf stories. (Zipes, *Trials and Tribulations*, 20.)
47. Zipes, *Trials and Tribulations*, 91.
48. Perrault translated by Zipes, *Trials and Tribulations*, 91.
49. Perrault translated by Zipes, *Trials and Tribulations*, 93.
50. Grimms translated by Zipes, *Trials and Tribulations*, 135.
51. *Ibid.*
52. Grimms translated by Zipes, *Trials and Tribulations*, 135-9.
53. In her study on childbirth in fairytales in early modern France, Holly Tucker argues that 'a woman's identity centered on her ability to marry and to procreate' (*Pregnant Fictions: Childbirth And The Fairy Tale In Early Modern France* (Michigan: Wayne State University Press, 2003), 1). Furthermore, it was not uncommon for aristocratic mothers to be the chief educators of their underage children (Gibson, *Women In Seventeenth-Century France*, 142). Pregnancy and infertility were recurrent themes in many 17th-century fairy tales (Tucker, *Pregnant Fictions*, 8). This reflected the importance of motherhood and procreation in relation to

continuing the family line.

54. Foucault, *Discipline and Punish*, 25.
55. Annette Iggulden, 'Silent Speech' in E. Barret and B. Bolt (eds), *Practice as Research: Approaches to Creative Arts Enquiry*, 4th edn (London and New York: I.B Tauris & Co., 2010), 65-6.
56. Lieberman, 'Some Day My Prince Will Come', 194.
57. Warner, *From the Beast to the Blonde*, 29.
58. Warner, *From the Beast to the Blonde*, 50.
59. Perrault translated by Zipes, *Trials and Tribulations*, 93.
60. Zipes, *Trials and Tribulations*, 80.
61. Zipes, *Trials and Tribulations*, 77.
62. Zipes, *Trials and Tribulations*, 80.
63. Zipes, *Trials and Tribulations*, 8.
64. Zipes, *Trials and Tribulations*, 27.
65. *Ibid*.
66. Zipes, *Trials and Tribulations*, 27 and 55.
67. Zipes, *Trials and Tribulations*, 25.
68. Delarue first published 'The Story of Grandmother' in the journal *Bulletin Folklorique d'Ill-de-France* in 1951 (Delarue, 'Les Contes merveilleux de Perrault', 221). Among his research (which included 35 oral versions of the Little Red Riding Hood narratives) was his transcription of an 1885 manuscript he discovered in Nievre, France. Zipes and other academics (such as Orenstein) argue that Delarue's transcription is a truer version of the 17th-century oral tale than Perrault's 1695 narrative (Zipes, *Trials and Tribulations*, 4; Orenstein, *Little Red Riding Hood Uncloaked*, 75). This is due to the unique story motifs which are absent in Perrault's literary version, i.e. the 'paths of pins and needles, the blood of granny, the defecation in bed and the escape of the girl' (Zipes, *Trials and Tribulations*, 4 and 25). Similar oral versions were also recorded by Charles Joisten in the south of France during the 1950s (Zipes, *Trials and Tribulations*, 6). However, Zipes' repeated use of the phrase 'original oral tale' in reference to Delarue's 20th-century text is problematic as it is impossible to confirm which oral versions circulated in 17th-century France. Ruth Bottigheimer (*Fairy Tales: A New History* (Albany: State University of New York Press, 2009), 54) and Jan Ziolkowski ('A Fairy Tale from before Fairy Tales', *Speculum*, 551) argue that Perrault's 1695 literary fairy tale is the existing pre-text and an original story created from an amalgamation of medieval texts and ancient fables. This notion is supported by Dundes ('Introduction', *Little Red Riding Hood: A Casebook*, 3) and several other scholars cited in Carole Hanks and D.T. Hanks, 'Perrault's "Little Red Riding Hood": Victim of the Revisers', *Children's Literature*, vol. 7 (1978): 68-77, http://muse.jhu.edu.ezproxy-f.deakin.edu.au/article/245962 (i.e. Maria Leach, *Dictionary of Folklore, Mythology, and Legend* (New York: Funk and Wagnalls, 1949); Geoffrey Brereton, *Perrault's Fairy Tales* (Penguin, 1957); Jaques Barchilon and Henry Pettit, *The Authentic Mother Goose Fairy Tales and Nursery Rhymes* (Denver: Alan Swallow, 1960); Stith Thompson, *One Hundred Favorite Folktales* (Bloomington and London: Indiana Univ. Press, 1968); and Iona and Peter Opie, *The Classic Fairy Tales* (London: Oxford Univ. Press, 1974)).
69. Zipes, *Trials and Tribulations*, xi & 7-8.
70. Zipes, *Trials and Tribulations*, 8.
71. Zipes, *Trials and Tribulations*, 13.
72. Zipes, *Trials and Tribulations*, 11.
73. Foucault, *Discipline and Punish*, 103.
74. Bettelheim, *The Uses of Enchantment*, 176.
75. Foucault, *Discipline and Punish*, 109.
76. Orenstein, *Little Red Riding Hood Uncloaked*, 22.
77. Orenstein, *Little Red Riding Hood Uncloaked*, 23.
78. Orenstein, *Little Red Riding Hood Uncloaked*, 26.

79. *Ibid.*
80. Jack Zipes, 'A Second Gaze at Little Red Riding Hood's Trials and Tribulations', *The Lion and the Unicorn*, vol. 7/8 (1983-4), 93.
81. Zipes, 'A Second Gaze', 91 and 92.
82. Zipes, A Second Gaze', 80.
83. *Ibid.*
84. *Ibid.*
85. Bettelheim, *Uses Of Enchantment*, 169; Zipes, *Trials and Tribulations*, 27 and 33; F.W.N. Bailey in Zipes, *Trials and Tribulations*, 158.
86. Michel Foucault, *Discipline and Punish*, 101.
87. Nina Strochli, 'Famed "Afghan Girl" Finally Gets a Home', *National Geographic*, 13 December 2017, https://www.nationalgeographic.com/pages/article/afghan-girl-home-afghanistan (accessed 8 April 2021).
88. Karen Percy and staff, 'Eurydice Dixon's killer Jaymes Todd jailed for life for her rape and murder', ABC News, 2 September 2019, https://www.abc.net.au/news/2019-09-02/eurydice-dixon-killer-jaymes-todd-sentenced/11469328 (accessed 17 March 2021).
89. Verdier, 'Little Red Riding Hood in Oral Tradition', 106.
90. Zipes, *Trials and Tribulations*, 24.
91. Delarue, 'Les Contes merveilleux de Perrault', 232.
92. Zipes, *Trials and Tribulations*, 7 and 25.
93. Delarue, 'Les Contes merveilleux de Perrault', 221.
94. Delarue translated by Zipes, *Trials and Tribulations*, 22.
95. *Ibid.*
96. Delarue, 'Les Contes merveilleux de Perrault', 221.
97. Foucault, *Discipline and Punish*, 44.
98. Foucault, *Discipline and Punish*, 35-6.
99. Paul Delarue, *The Borzoi Book of French Folk Tales*, trans. Austin E. Fife (USA: Alfred A. Knopf, 1956), 231.
100. Delarue, *The Borzoi Book Of French Folk Tales*, 231.
101. Foucault, *Discipline and Punish*, 61.
102. Foucault, *Discipline and Punish*, 27.

FREE Fairy Tale Workshop

with
Purchase of Sophia's Tale
& 5 Star Amazon Review

Saturday 3 July

WEB: drsarahwalton.com/fairytale-workshop
EMAIL: sarahsoulwriting@gmail.com

A FAIRY TALE REVOLUTION

Cinderella Liberator

REBECCA SOLNIT

46

Once Upon a 'Fairy Tale Revolution': Adapting Canonical Fairy Tales Beyond Happily Ever After

Michelle Anya Anjirbag

T he staying power of the fairy tale as a genre relies on its transformative potential, its endless potential to be always remade to meet the needs of the current world, creating a continuum of story and dialogue between past and present. As Cristina Bacchilega notes, 'the multiplicity of fairy-tale versions and the multivocality of the genre offer a fertile opportunity for intervening in an already multi-layered reflection on story, social practices, and cultural values'.[1] Likewise, Maria Tatar notes that 'the pleasures of the genre arouse curiosity about the world around us and provide social, cultural, and intellectual capital for navigating its perils. For that reason, fairy tales have been credited with an insurrectionary and emancipatory potential'.[2] The two critics here both highlight the social and cultural positioning of the genre and its potential to provoke new ways of viewing the world, as products of the tales' historical contexts.

The new 'Fairy Tale Revolution' series from the Penguin Random House's Vintage Children's Classics imprint seizes on this transformative impulse, commissioning new tales 'with compassion and freedom at their core'.[3] The books are marketed as reinventions, remixes and updates, specifically for children: *Hansel and Greta* by Jeanette Winterson, *Cinderella Liberator* by Rebecca Solnit, *Duckling* by Kamila Shamsie, and *Blueblood* by Malorie Blackman. These picture books were published in the UK in late 2020, and three of them are due to be published in the US in late 2021 (Rebecca Solnit's *Cinderella Liberator* is available in the US at the time of writing, published in 2019 by Haymarket Books). But though the marketing emphasises compassion and freedom, the 'revolutionary' nature of these texts is really the transformation of the concept of the 'happy ending' – something Marina Warner identifies as characterising the wonder tale[4] – each of them moving away from the individual's happiness or transcendence of their situation, and towards a happily ever after as a greater sense of justice, or the potential to build a more just world, with resolutions that are more attainable than acts of magic and wonder. Together, these books indicate a new direction for the transformation of the genre, and the evolution of both the fairy tale itself and the concept of what makes a 'happy ending' after all.

Imagine 'Hansel and Gretel' but where food insecurity and greed is replaced with the evils of capitalist conspicuous consumption and resource-grabbing, and the resolution involves a rejection of that mode of contemporary life. Or 'The Ugly Duckling', but at the end the duckling realises not that they are beautiful, but that they are more than their appearance to others. Or a retelling of 'Bluebeard' where there is no enchanted key, but in which abusive men are brought to their knees. Or maybe a version of 'Cinderella' that questions child labour and argues for dignity in work to liberate everyone. These are postmodern retellings, descendants of writers such as Margaret Atwood, Anne Sexton and Angela Carter, providing a 'revised magic'[5] that does 'more than alter our reading of these narratives. Like metafolklore, they constitute an ideological test for previous interpretations and in doing so, postmodern fairy tales exhibit an awareness of how the folktale, which modern humans relegate to the nursery, almost vindictively patterns our unconscious'.[6] This patterning can also be thought of as what Maria Tatar calls 'palimpsestic memory, a vibrant process of building and demolishing, all the while leaving traces of the stories antecedent to the new telling'.[7]

This 'fairy tale revolution' plays with both the patterns of folktales and the conventions of illustrated fairy-tale books from the golden age of children's picture books. Three of the texts are accompanied by illustrations commissioned from Laura Barrett to coordinate with the Arthur Rackham silhouettes paired with Rebecca Solnit's 'Cinderella' retelling, connecting the past and the present. They are then further tied together with covers designed by Anna Morrison, who creates continuity across the series with bold colours and silhouettes reflecting the style of the illustrations within and the narratives themselves. Just as Warner notes that it was women who 'consciously invented the modern fairy tale',[8] these four female authors are consciously disrupting the fairy tale as it has been known, witnessed by the author's 'Afterword' at the end of each book explaining their individual inspirations and intentions with their recreations. As such they can be considered intertextual, critical interventions, recollecting Vanessa Joosen's critical work[9] realised creatively and contemporarily: in dialogue not with fairy-tale criticism, but openly critical in an unabashed, unapologetic way of contemporary conditions. The open criticism is part of these retellings.

Bacchilega defines a postmodern fairy tale as 'characterized by a double movement of exposure: one that reveals the ideological framing of women in the most popular fairy tales and another that makes visible or activates unexploited or forgotten possibilities in these well-known stories'.[10] While satisfying retellings alone, together these texts reinvent the canonical fairy tale for the contemporary reader, specifically as framed by female voices. These authors remake the tales to fit modern audiences, inviting as works of postmodern adaptation a new take on the dangers of the present as part of a continuum of timeless ills such as food insecurity, domestic violence and discrimination. Hansel and Gretel's story becomes transformed through the much larger implications of global climate crisis; Bluebeard's control of his wife, and his violent murders of his past wives, are reinterpreted into a tale where the consequences of vengeance are realised rather than glorified; the duckling finds hope in a cruel world, but the plight of the outsider has remained and become exacerbated; Cinderella becomes liberated from her two choices of marriage or servitude, and liberates others along with herself. The pursuit of a more just world puts these tales in dialogue with not only the postmodern retellings from the 1970s onwards, but the tradition of *les précieuses* and their successors – educated women in 17th-century France using the genre to argue for more equal and just treatment[11] – making them books that overtly deploy politics of both wonder and intertextuality to generate their commentary, literary acts of both critical and creative adaptation.

Cinderella Liberator by Rebecca Solnit is perhaps retold the closest to its originating tale, while also greatly expanding the narrative. Though fidelity is a somewhat meaningless metric of the value of an adaptation, especially when considering fairy tales and folklore, it is worth mentioning here because of how the series as a whole deploys, or does not deploy, wonder or magic in its resolutions. In her Afterword, Solnit writes about being struck by the scene of the transformation of pumpkin and mice into coach and horses, not just the magic itself, but 'Cinderella's active collaboration in bringing about the metamorphosis'.[12] In identifying this as a 'story about transformation, not just about getting your prince', as well as other relationships,[13] Solnit centres at her transformation of the text itself the question of 'how to preserve something of the charm of transformation and the plight of the child, and how to work out a more palatable exit from her plight than the one we all know'.[14]

Solnit's version decouples the idea of virtue from one's self-worth, honours the working child 'without kindness or security in their everyday lives',[15] and disrupts the assumption that marriage is a route to a woman's finding herself. She writes, reflecting on the story she created, that 'it seemed to me that the solution to overwork and degrading work is not the leisure of a princess, passing off the work to others, but good, meaningful work with dignity and self-determination'.[16] Solnit makes the story more about the stepmother's control, which moves the story to a frame of liberation beyond Cinderella's alone, and redresses the idea that beauty has anything to do with someone's intrinsic worth: agency and purpose can be revolutionary.

In *Cinderella Liberator*, the stepsisters are renamed Pearlita and Paloma (the Prince is also renamed from Charming to Nevermind). The stepmother remains unnamed, but from the beginning it is clear that Pearlita and Paloma are also oppressed in this narrative, as Solnit writes that the stepmother 'wanted a lot for her own two daughters … (Nobody asked what Cinderella or Pearlita or Paloma wanted)'.[17] Cinderella was able to interact with townspeople and so she 'became a good cook. She got to know everyone in the marketplace. She grew strong and capable'.[18] In comparison, 'Pearlita and Paloma sat upstairs trying on clothes and arranging their hair and not going out, because the people in the town were not fancy enough for them, according to their mother'.[19] Solnit removes the dichotomy of beauty and virtue layered into other versions of the story, most notably permeating the

49

popular imagination in modernity via Disney's cinematic adaptations of 1950 and 2015. By doing this she removes the taint of ugliness and its automatic condemnation from the stepsisters and also frees Cinderella from the implications of beauty as her only gift, highlighting her skills and capabilities.

The commentary on beauty is made more explicit when Paloma and Pearlita are getting ready for the ball, to which Cinderella has not been invited. The stepsisters are concerned with what they think will make them beautiful, but the narrative text shows that the sisters are constricted as well: 'their ballgowns [...] were so long and tight they couldn't have run after a dog or climbed a fence. They were not sure they were beautiful, but they were sure that being beautiful would make them happy.'[20]

On the same page, two paragraphs higher, Solnit dedicates the longest paragraph of text to explaining, 'But there isn't actually a most beautiful person in the world, because there are so many kinds of beauty', and goes on to describe many different versions of what might be found beautiful.[21] The text frames a black silhouette of Cinderella in her rags, while the facing page depicts Cinderella sitting on a stool, a line of rags drying about over her head, crying into a handkerchief. This discourse about love and beauty, and the accompanying illustration, highlight Cinderella's neglect, abandonment and loneliness, and also undermine the connections between beauty, self-worth and happiness held over from antecedent versions. The stepsisters are not evil here, but they are not happy. They cannot tell if they are beautiful or not, nor have they been shown another way to find their own sense of self-worth. Cinderella, too, cannot find happiness in her situation, because she is neglected and alone, but without a path to an improved situation.

The introduction of the fairy godmother and the scenes of transformation, the ball and the lost slipper unfold much as expected before the real disruptions to the narrative begin. The fairy godmother is waiting for Cinderella when she returns home, and passes on the lesson that 'true magic is to help each thing become its best and most free self',[22] before asking all of the transformed animals if they would like to be turned back to what they were or not. In this way, Solnit centres both agency and consent: the power of choice and right to self-determination extends to servants and animals. The Prince does search for Cinderella, but not to offer marriage. He does it because he 'was a very polite person, and he was sad he had frightened his guest and she had lost her shoe'.[23] Marriage is not the goal for either the prince or Cinderella in this narrative, and he too becomes more rounded a character with feelings and agency. Cinderella identifies herself as the owner of the slipper while her stepsisters are trying it on. This is the moment that Solnit pushes her disruption of the known 'Cinderella' narrative into a liberating reimagining, as the story's resolution is achieved through Cinderella's own agency. She provides a counternarrative to what it means to have wealth, stating that 'there is always enough for everyone, if you share it properly, or if it has been shared properly before you got there',[24] the use of 'you' addressing the reader directly, outside of the frame of the narrative itself. The fairy godmother returns to provide further commentary, prophecy and backstory: this Cinderella is not the Disneyfied orphan;[25] her father is a judge 'who had to go far away to help others and thought his new wife and her daughters would be kind' and her mother is 'a great sea captain, who lost her ship at sea and will come home one day on another ship'.[26] Instead of the implication of a marriage and a new family, this Cinderella will be restored to the family she thought she had lost.

Where other versions of Cinderella end with the Prince finding her, or the punishment of the stepfamily, Solnit instead chooses to write new endings for everyone: Cinderella has a cake shop, Pearlita runs a hair salon, Paloma is a seamstress, and the stepmother becomes the 'roaring in the trees on stormy nights … saying *More and more and more* …'[27] In Solnit's telling, 'they became their truest selves'.[28] In the end, Cinderella gets to reclaim her name, Ella, as the final word of the story. By writing past the known end of a well-known fairy tale, Solnit seizes the potential of fairy-tale retellers to comment on society and call for change, most notably in line with postmodern feminist fairy-tale writers. Jack Zipes notes that writers such as Carter and Sexton were revolutionary not because they 'break with the past' but rather because their work reflects a pattern of 'working through, absorbing, and elaborating the past'.[29] He continues:

> One of the important political purposes of women's writing of fairy tales was to demonstrate that nobody lived happily ever after the fairy tale seemingly ended, whether in fantasy or reality, and nobody will ever live happily ever after unless we change not only fairy-tale writing but social and economic conditions that further exploitative relations among the sexes, races, and social classes. This general purpose is still at the root of the best and most serious writing of fairy tales by women …[30]

Solnit seizes on this purpose, imagining new conditions where happiness might be realised, liberating both characters and readers alike.

Kamila Shamsie's *Duckling* also draws on themes of liberation, opening up Hans Christian Andersen's 'The Ugly Duckling' as a narrative of personal acceptance, but also about 'what happens when an outsider enters a homogenous world that is hostile to difference – and then what happens when that same outsider finds "her own tribe" again'.[31] Though the frame and scope of Shamsie's narrative remains far closer to Andersen's version than Solnit's did to other versions of 'Cinderella', it differs greatly in terms of the titular character's internal life, and how those thoughts are presented to readers as motivating the duckling's actions throughout the narrative. Shamsie reinvents 'The Ugly Duckling', dropping the 'ugly', changing the genders of several characters (the duckling becomes female, the old female duck in the barnyard becomes the male Grand Old Duck, among others) and deliberately layering kindness throughout the narrative. In this version, the mother duck is kind to the duckling until her fear of expulsion from the safety of the barnyard wins out over her care for the child, and she too acts cruelly to her. The duckling sets off on her own, meeting many other creatures on her way, including two young goslings who call themselves adventurers and invite her to join them, before hunters disturb them. The duckling continues to travel, and suffer, until after a hard winter she asks herself, 'Is it better, perhaps, to risk cruelty if it also means taking a chance on kindness?'[32] This leads her to meet the swans who accept her, and this is where Shamsie, like Solnit, writes past the end of the antecedent tale, tapping into an 'improvisational energy [that] has always kept the fairy tale alive. Tellers walk down familiar paths but can branch off into new territory'.[33] Andersen's story ends with the Ugly Duckling's joy at his acceptance by the swans; Shamsie's story takes readers back to the beginning, returning the Egyptian stork who begins both tales but never appears again in Andersen's version. The duckling, who is now accepted by her own kind, observes those who accept her rejecting someone else for being different, when the stork returns looking for help to find the 'raincloud duck'.[34] The duckling is reunited with her mother and the two goslings who were kind to her. The swans first refuse to help, and then both the swans and the mother duck fight over who and what the duckling is. Shamsie's retelling closes with the duckling's declaration that she is 'an adventurer' and the closing narration line of 'Then she turned and looked at the geese, at the duck, at the stork, at the swans and at you who are reading this story. "Who's coming with me?" she said'.[35] Shamsie breaks the fourth wall and invites readers to also seize control of their own identities and determine for themselves who they are and who they will become, as well as how they will treat others.

Hansel and Greta by Jeanette Winterson takes a wider look at the world, retelling 'Hansel and Gretel' with an ecocritical, climate justice-oriented bent. The title includes an allusion to activist Greta Thunberg, and Winterson writes in her Afterword about 'all-consuming greed on the loose'[36] as a point of departure for her retelling. In this version, Gretel becomes Greta, and she, her brother Hansel who can talk to trees, and their dad (a lumberjack only referred to as Dad) live '[d]eep in the wood' with their dead mother's big sister GreedyGuts, who is 'at least 10 feet tall and 5 feet wide' and might be an ogre.[37] Greta's narration relates how her father works in the woods cutting down trees to clear space for a high-speed railway, and how GreedyGuts consumes food and resources insatiably. One day Greta's father decides destroying the forest is making him sad, so the family start planting trees in the forest to replace those being cut down and he eventually quits his job. From the outset, Winterson's version of the fairy tale questions the cost of so-called progress, drawing attention to what is lost in the face of technological improvements such as high-speed rail. While GreedyGuts is away in the city visiting her friend GuzzleGuts, Greta, Hansel and their dad start living more sustainably, planting a garden, raising chickens for eggs, and fishing, this version of the story becoming an unabashedly ecocritical revision of the fairy tale. Winterson's call for sustainability is put in direct contrast to GreedyGuts' worldview where 'the point of life is to eat as much as possible [and] make as much money as possible.[38] Eventually Dad goes to the city to find work to support GreedyGuts' consumption. She then has Dad's ex-boss (BeardFace) drop Hansel and Greta in the middle of a destroyed part of the woods where they have never been before, near an abandoned house, a rhetorical move that absolves Hansel and Greta's father of his active abandonment of his children in antecedent versions. Hansel and Greta meet a Little Tree, who tells them about the Witch in the Wood who had been driven out of the woods by the bulldozers. The three make their way back home to try to call their dad and tell him what has happened, but find their house occupied by GreedyGuts, GuzzleGuts, BeardFace, and his brother BogFace. The children and Little Tree are then abandoned in the city by BogFace who says, 'Now go and get a job and don't come back until you've made a million pounds',[39] reiterating the consumerist values that Winterson villainises through the narrative. The children then meet a lady in a park with 'a pointy nose, lots of black hair, only two teeth, and her eyes were red',[40] who offers to help them with the caveat that they 'don't eat her house'.[41] This is, in fact, the Little Tree's friend, the Witch of the Wood. She lives in a Gingerbread House in a compound that can only be accessed by ticketholders. She has been put there by GuzzleGuts, and the gingerbread is not made of 'normal sugar and normal chocolate and normal cake. It's a special recipe – and when you eat it, all you want is to eat more and more and more.'[42] GuzzleGuts sells this Evil Gingerbread through her website and gets rich; the witch is stuck as part of a type of 'Santa's Grotto thing' where 'kids come to see the wicked witch'.[43] The Witch is not an evil figure in and of herself, but has been forced to fit into a capitalist narrative. Winterson's version is especially unique in how it treats the figure of the stepmother who urges the abandonment of the children in the wood, and the figure of the witch who wants to eat children. Evil is shifted away from the witch and onto the capitalist construct that GreedyGuts and her friends represent: all-consuming consumption with no thought of what is destroyed in the process. The witch takes Hansel and Greta to find their dad, and they make a plan to defeat GreedyGuts and GuzzleGuts. They all return to the house in the woods. BeardFace and BogFace are turned into frogs, and GreedyGuts is exposed as an ogre (GuzzleGuts has already died, suffocated by her own clothing). The witch then removes the fake teeth and the red contacts and introduces herself as Ruby, saying that the children have freed her from 'My own spell! The ones you cast on yourself are the really scary ones. I believed I had no power left. Just a life of Evil Gingerbread.'[44] They plant the Little Tree in their garden, and Dad proposes elopement to Ruby who answers, 'You're not so bad, Mr. Dad, but we have to get to know each other first and see how the children feel about it all',[45] and the book ends on them all living 'happily ever after' in the wood together. The resolution of Winterson's narrative reaffirms the agency of its protagonists and calls into question the idea of marriage as the end goal of one's self-realisation, much like Shamsie's and Solnit's own retellings do in their own ways,[46] but with the added implication that the agency of the planet, here represented in the forest and the trees that Hansel can speak to, also needs consideration and recognition.

Blueblood by Malorie Blackman is perhaps the most postmodern of the retellings, stepping furthest away from its originating story, and consciously asking 'In fighting back against that which we deplore, how do we stop ourselves from becoming deplorable? ... can the ends ever justify the means?'[47] Not only does technology replace the magic of 'Bluebeard,' it is written as both an allusive retelling and a continuation of Bluebeard's own story, and the resolution does not celebrate the vigilante justice of the narrative, but rather acknowledges that all violence, including that in the pursuit of justice, has a price. In this way, *Blueblood* embraces the legacy of postmodernism, 'the blurring of boundaries between fiction and criticism, a blurring that depends both on intertextuality and self-conscious reflexivity',[48] or as Blackman puts it, it's 'a modern-day retelling with a viper's twist in the tale'.[49]

Blueblood moves between the third-person omniscient perspectives of Nia and her husband Marcus. The only other characters named are Nia's brothers Jakob and Desmond, who predominantly feature in the first chapter as protesting her plans to marry Marcus. Marcus is fifteen years older than Nia, has a 'thick and crusty-looking' beard,[50] and 'shifty eyes, all the better to constantly watch you with'.[51] Nia marries him anyway, despite her brothers' concerns and other 'rumours',[52] and the perspective switches to focus on Marcus's point of view for the duration of the next chapter. When embedded in his perspective, readers find out that there is also 'malicious gossip' centred around Nia regarding a previous marriage and a husband who had run off and left her,[53] and that Marcus feels unsettled by Nia's success and wealth as a jewellery designer. He will be moving into her house with the request that she will stay out of his space in the attic he needs to stay out of her studio in the basement. These first two chapters allude to versions of 'Bluebeard': a woman marrying a much older man, mention of a beard that is 'so black, in certain lights it looks almost midnight blue',[54] rumours about past spouses, and forbidden rooms, but with a different dynamic as he has moved into her house, and she has forbidden certain rooms to him. Over the course of the text, Marcus becomes more jealous and controlling, demanding to see her studio and be with her whenever she goes out. Nia leaves for a business trip, and he decides to look for the entrance to the basement, not knowing that she had installed cameras around the house to see if he would betray her and intrude on her space – the cameras replacing the magical key or egg from the antecedent versions. He finds his way in, thinking Nia is still away on her trip for a few more days, not knowing she is waiting inside, and not ready for the secret she is keeping: human ears in hermetically sealed display cases, 'from an ex-husband and others, bullies like you who were too arrogant and full of themselves to listen'.[55]

This is Blackman's 'vipers' twist; Nia is the descendant of Aloysius Barbleue: Nia Bluebeard. She explains: 'It's ironic that I follow in his footsteps while trying to atone for what he did to so many women'.[56] She enacts a vigilante justice against Marcus, who has had three previous wives, two who divorced him and one who died before she could, and whose other relationships required police intervention due to 'controlling, bullying, emotional and physical abuse',[57] who has never been touched by the law because of his High Court Judge mother.[58] Marcus's ear is added to her collection. But the book does not end on a heroic note. Blackman's narrator does not condone Nia's actions. The last scene sees her sitting in the study looking at her favourite wedding photo, realising 'she'd become the very thing she abhorred' and resolving that 'there would be no more husbands, no more partnerships. And when her time finally came, she would come down to this basement, disable the lift – and never leave. That would be her punishment and her penance.'[59]

Maria Tatar notes that 'fairy tales are always more interesting when something is added to them … each new retelling recharges the narrative, making it crackle and hiss with cultural energy'.[60] Blackman's appropriation of 'Bluebeard' – in the sense of appropriation as a text that 'effects a more decisive journey away from the informing text into a wholly new cultural product and domain, often through the acts of interpolation and critique as much as through the movement from one genre to others'[61] – asks what is worse, a serial killer or a domestic abuser, and valorises neither in the resolution, managing also to include a subtle indictment of a justice system that protects abusers. There is something stunning about reading this text against the backdrops of the #MeToo movement and the Sarah Everard case and protests, women sharing their encounters with abuse, protesting the same issues over several decades with no real change, and the knowledge that what Blackman presents in this postmodern retelling is not a fairy tale in the sense of encapsulating a moment of wonder, but rather an impossible wish fulfilment: what if a woman *could* take her revenge against one of the most banal evils of the world past, present, and probably future. Tatar writes that 'much of the magic of fairy tales derives from their mutability',[62] but there is no happy ending or magic here, no riding away from the controlling, abusive husband, no brothers coming in to save Nia. Nia saves herself, saves other women, but to do so outside the boundaries of a system that has, in the case of Marcus, protected a known abuser, Nia is the one who has become the serial killer – not a hero. And she knows that she too must face a form of justice. There can be no magic, no happy endings for women facing a persistent, systemic evil as old as time.

Especially considering the themes, the twist, and the lack of a 'happy ending' in *Blueblood*, it might seem curious that the form of the picture book, something associated with and marketed specifically to and for children, was the format of choice for Vintage's 'Fairy Tale Revolution'. The idea of fairy-tale versions, especially as more and more cinematic versions are produced, provokes ideas of limitless possibilities. In contrast, these are limited to a textual length of 32 pages, and adorned with very simple, if bold, single-coloured silhouetted illustrations. *Cinderella Liberator* only features shades of blue, whereas *Blueblood* is dominated by red, *Hansel and Greta* by shades of green, and *Duckling* by yellow. The strict page count of a commercial picture book format and the bold but sparse colour scheme seem like they should serve to constrict imagination, as there is very little detail provided, or room for embellishment. Likewise, the peritext of the Afterword in each book guides and shapes interpretation of the preceding narrative instead of leaving it up to the individual reader. It is rare to have simultaneously subversive and didactic authorial intentions so explicitly provided, even if traditionally fairy tale collections were also shaped by various intentions – to domesticate, to instruct, to build nations, and to criticise the directions in which societies might be headed. In some ways, the confines of the picture book form make apparent the inherent contradictions in the adaptation of fairy tales to new contexts: the dual impetuses of subversion and didacticism, and the audience these stories are aimed at – the children to whom the picture book is marketed, or the adults who choose to purchase these books. Maria Tatar notes that 'Fairy tales, rather than sending messages, teaching morals, or constructive lessons, get conversations going. Piling on one outrage after another, they oblige us to react, to take positions and make judgements, enabling us to work through cultural contradiction using the power of a symbolic story',[63] highlighting not the instructive use of the fairy tale genre, but its capacity to serve as a mirror for the world and its 'outrages', provoking reaction from its audience. And yet Marina Warner's observation that, especially perhaps when it comes to these modern picture books, 'the fairy way of writing packaged and pictured for younger readers, become a mode of communicating moral values, political dreams, and even scientific knowledge',[64] also holds true, as these books are openly didactic, addressing the reader directly with instructions for how to navigate their world, providing mandates for what a more just world might look like. These two statements become unified in the picture book because, as noted by Nathalie op de Beeck, in the picture book format, 'content and form are intertwined', yielding almost the 'ideal format ... to express the fairy tale of modernity'.[65] Where op de Beeck is writing about the role of picture books in constructing the mythos of postwar society and progress, it is a statement that extends to fairy tales adapted in other times and contexts.[66] Ergo, the structure of the physical picture book and the narrative function of the fairy-tale form combine to draw paratextual ties between old stories in their multiple versions and new iterations, unlocking a new sense of wonder to be rediscovered. The silhouettes in the Fairy Tale Revolution series tap into the symbolic power of the fairy tale and, where they might lack illustrative detail, their shadows in some ways recall the shadows of past versions. That GreedyGuts is an ogre is shown through the images, as is the Duckling's many encounters with other animals, and even the tension between Nia and Marcus. By eliding the various violences of the text with symbolic images, a space is created for conversations, for 'outrages' to be reacted to. These books are direct in their lessons – not with directives nor concluding morals in verse-form, but consequences for behaving in unjust or harmful ways.

Postmodern feminist adaptations often unlock the darker potential of fairy tales away from the nursery they had been consigned to, and move the genre 'along a different path, producing creative adaptations that unsettle the genre by breaking with tradition and renewing it'.[67] These picture books, too, are in dialogue with both the fairy tale canon and female-authored fairy tale adaptations as counter-texts,[68] written against the normative gender, social and cultural hierarchies of their day. The depth achieved by featuring four female writers of various backgrounds, each taking on a particular kind of contemporary injustice or violence to assert that 'it need not continue',[69] recalls Warner's assertion that 'it is worth trying to puzzle out in what different ways the patterns of fairytale romancing might be drawn when women are the tellers'.[70] Changes to the traditional tales are deliberate, weighted, with intention to affect how the narrative is received and what is taken from it. As noted above, there is a sense of a didactic or pedagogic function to these four books, in part because of the form of the fairy-tale picture book and in part because of the peritext of the Afterword. As Warner writes:

> The pedagogical function of the wonder story deepens the sympathy between the social category women occupy and fairy tale. Fairy tales exchange knowledge between the older voice of experience and a younger audience, they present pictures of perils and possibilities that lie ahead, they use terror to set limits on choice and offer consolation to the wronged, they draw social outlines around boys and girls, fathers and mothers, the rich and the poor, the rulers and the ruled, they point out the evildoers and garland the virtuous, they stand up to adversity with dreams of vengeance, power and vindication.[71]

The authors of these four retellings participate in this knowledge exchange, making visible evils of the contemporary world and providing resolutions. It is in their resolutions that these books might be considered revolutionary, both in terms of what they impart, and in how they might indicate a direction in which the genre might be remade.

For all the changes in each story, the endings of these retellings are the most divergent from antecedent canonical versions. The 'happy ending' has become one of the most recognisable components of fairy tales – it is what is implied when people mention 'fairy tale weddings' or when fashion shoots draw from fairy tale iconography to create luxury tableaus.[72] The implication is that there is a story, and it is going to end happily, with wealth, fortune, and ease for those involved in the story, which has transcended the mundane, brought a sense of wonder into the world, and might just be also attainable for everyday people. This commercialised fairy-tale ending can be tied to many different cultural narratives from Hollywood to the fairy-tale canon where wonder and enchantment lead to changed circumstances for protagonists. However, despite being themselves commercial projects as published picture books, it is revolutionary that these four retellings together abandoned that concept for an ending, whether writing past the antecedent versions' endings or changing the parameters for what constitutes happiness.

These narratives choose instead, as consciously described in the Afterwords, structures of contentment, agency, and justice over unattainable utopian bliss. For example, Solnit writes at the end of her Afterword that 'this book is also with love and hope for liberation for every child who's overworked and undervalued, every kid who feels alone – with hope that they get to write their own story, and make it come out with love and liberation'.[73] Here love is not a romantic love; the liberated Ella learns to love and honour herself above all. Shamsie's Duckling chooses to define herself not as a duck or a swan, but as an adventurer, neither relying on others' definitions of who she is to validate her, nor choosing to close her world to new relationships and experiences. Blackman's Nia ends her story in sadness, but also on the note that two wrongs do not actually make a right, highlighting the danger of becoming the thing one hates under the banner of serving deserved justice. Winterson's witch, Ruby, does not believe in the romance of elopement as her route to 'happily ever after', but rather defines it as knowing exactly who one is and how powerful they are, and believing that one can change the world. The retellings together encourage readers, especially those reading in dialogue with antecedent versions they already know, to ask what is happiness, but also, what is security, where does it come from, and can everyone have it? They raise questions of belonging and community while reaffirming individuals' power and agency to remake their understandings of the world and their place in it, and changing the lives of others. They address very real contemporary evils, crises, and modes of existence, while also placing limits on behaviour, asserting that, while there is always a choice of how to act, all choices have consequences.

In his study of the remaking of the fairy tale in relation to childhood, Zipes cites Ernst Bloch's insistence that 'the fairy tale would always address what is lacking in society and would illuminate a better future'.[74] Arguably, these retellings do exactly that, but illuminating options for a better present – the ideas of liberation for those working without kindness, dignity, or security, of living more consciously regarding the effects of consumption on the planet, of being aware of domestic violence as a real and contemporary problem, of how to see and break cycles of xenophobia, can all be acted upon now. And even with the albeit at times heavy-handed didacticism of the narratorial voice, these retellings encapsulate Tatar's description of being 'to double duty bound, entertaining and provoking, and above all ensuring that a culture of silence cannot descend on us'.[75] The uniting, revolutionary thread through all of these is a refusal to be silent or meek in the face of injustice. If part of the political purpose of female-voiced retellings is to show that 'no one will have a happy ending unless we change',[76] then these retellings specifically explicate how society might be changed, breaking from the emphasis on the patriarchal structures of marriage embedded in the canonical versions, and embracing newly imagined, transformative futures with more power vested in the individual's potential. With these new versions adding to the multivocality of the fairy tale genre, just like these authors, readers can retell old tales, remake old patterns into what they want to hear, and remake the world into what they want the world to be.

. . . .

Michelle Anya Anjirbag

Notes

1. Cristina Bacchilega, *Postmodern Fairy Tales: Gender and Narrative Strategy* (Philadelphia: University of Pennsylvania Press, 1994), 76.
2. Maria Tatar, *The Hard Facts of the Grimms' Fairy Tales: Expanded Edition* (Oxford: Princeton University Press, 2019 (2003)), xviii.
3. Penguin Books. 'Introducing A Fairy Tale Revolution', accessed 8 March 2021, https://www.penguin.co.uk/articles/2020/october/a-fairy-tale-revolution.html.
4. Marina Warner, *Wonder Tales: Six Stories of Enchantment* (London: Chatto & Windus, 1994), 6.
5. Bacchilega, *Postmodern Fairy Tales*, 141.
6. Bacchilega, *Postmodern Fairy Tales*, 22.
7. Tatar, *Hard Facts*, xix.
8. Warner, *Wonder Tales*, 4.
9. See Vanessa Joosen, *Critical & Creative Perspectives on Fairy Tales: An Intertextual Dialogue between Fairy-Tale Scholarship and Postmodern Retellings.* (Detroit: Wayne State UP, 2011).
10. Bacchilega, *Postmodern Fairy Tales*, 76.
11. Warner, *Wonder Tales*, 7.
12. Rebecca Solnit, *Cinderella Liberator* (London: Vintage Classics, 2020), 30.
13. *Ibid.*
14. *Ibid.*
15. *Ibid.*
16. *Ibid.*
17. Solnit, *Cinderella Liberator*, 3-4.
18. Solnit, *Cinderella Liberator*, 4.
19. *Ibid.*
20. Solnit, *Cinderella Liberator*, 6.
21. *Ibid.*
22. Solnit, *Cinderella Liberator*, 19.
23. Solnit, *Cinderella Liberator*, 21.
24. Solnit, *Cinderella Liberator*, 22.
25. Contemporary film adaptations, especially those made after the 1950 Disney animation, have followed a narrative of her father remarrying after her mother's death, and then her father dying so Cinderella is left under the control of the stepmother – the five 'A Cinderella Story' films made since 2004 and 'Ever After: A Cinderella Story' (1998) all follow this plot. The 2017 Disney live-action version also explicitly kills the father after the mother dies instead of just implying it, and there have also been about 30 other made-for-TV films from the Hallmark, Freeform, and ABC Family networks over the last 15 years that explicitly played with this concept, and in all cases kill off both of Cinderella's parents.
26. Solnit, *Cinderella Liberator*, 23.
27. Solnit, *Cinderella Liberator*, 27 (italics original).
28. *Ibid.*
29. Jack Zipes, *Relentless Progress: The Reconfiguration of Children's Literature, Fairy Tales, and Storytelling* (Abingdon: Routledge, 2009), 126.
30. Zipes, *Relentless Progress*, 129.

31. Kamila Shamsie, *Duckling* (London: Vintage Books, 2020), 31.

32. Shamsie, *Duckling*, 23.

33. Maria Tatar, *The Classic Fairy Tales*, 2nd edn (London: W.W. Norton & Company, 2017 (1999)), xv.

34. Shamsie, *Duckling*, 26.

35. Shamsie, *Duckling*, 30.

36. Jeanette Winterson, *Hansel and Greta* (London: Vintage Books, 2020), 31.

37. Winterson, *Hansel and Greta*, 2-3.

38. Winterson, *Hansel and Greta*, 11.

39. Winterson, *Hansel and Greta*, 21.

40. Winterson, *Hansel and Greta*, 22.

41. *Ibid*.

42. Winterson, *Hansel and Greta*, 24.

43. *Ibid*.

44. Winterson, *Hansel and Greta*, 29.

45. Winterson, *Hansel and Greta*, 30.

46. Shamsie, *Duckling*, 14; Solnit, *Cinderella Liberator*, 28.

47. Malorie Blackman, *Blueblood* (London: Vintage Books, 2020), 31.

48. Bacchilega, *Postmodern Fairy Tales*, 77.

49. Blackman, *Blueblood*, 31.

50. Blackman, *Blueblood*, 4.

51. *Ibid*.

52. Blackman, *Blueblood*, 6.

53. Blackman, *Blueblood*, 7.

54. *Ibid*.

55. Blackman, *Blueblood*, 25.

56. Blackman, *Blueblood*, 29.

57. Blackman, *Blueblood*, 25.

58. Blackman, *Blueblood*, 4, 25.

59. Blackman, *Blueblood*, 30.

60. Tatar, *The Classic Fairy Tales*, xiii.

61. Julie Sanders, *Adaptation and Appropriation*, 2nd edn (London: Routledge, 2016 (2006)), 35.

62. Maria Tatar, 'Introduction', *The Cambridge Companion to Fairy Tales*, ed. by Maria Tatar (Cambridge: Cambridge UP, 2015), 3.

63. *Ibid*.

64. Marina Warner, *Once Upon a Time: A Short History of Fairy Tale* (Oxford: Oxford UP, 2016), 109.

65. Nathalie op de Beeck, *Suspended Animation: Children's Picture Books and the Fairy Tale of Modernity* (Minneapolis: University of Minnesota Press, 2010), xvii.

66. Op de Beeck, *Suspended Animation*, 23.

67. Tatar, *The Classic Fairy Tales*, xix.

68. See Donald Haase (ed.), *Fairy Tales and Feminism: New Approaches* (Detroit: Wayne State UP, 2004)

69. Warner, *Once Upon a Time*, xxv.

70. Marina Warner, *From the Beast to the Blonde: On Fairy Tales and their Tellers* (London: Vintage, 1995), 21.

71. *Ibid*.

72. See Cristina Bacchilega, *Fairy Tales Transformed? Twenty-First-Century Adaptations and the Politics of Wonder* (Detroit: Wayne State UP, 2013).

73. Solnit, *Cinderella Liberator*, 31.

74. Zipes, *Relentless Progress*, 128.

75. Tatar, 'Introduction', *The Cambridge Companion to Fairy Tales*, 3.

76. Zipes, *Relentless Progress*, 129.

Poetry on the Lake

2nd Short Story competition: 1st Prize: €200.

Theme: *haunted*

An anthology of selected stories & poems will be printed, with authors' permission. Authors will receive a complimentary copy. Winner may read at October Celebration on Lake Orta, Italy.

Deadline: 31st July 2021. Any length,
but don't lose the judges' interest.
Fees: €12 first story, then €8

Contact: poetryonthelake@yahoo.co.uk
Info: https://www.poetryonthelake.org/competition

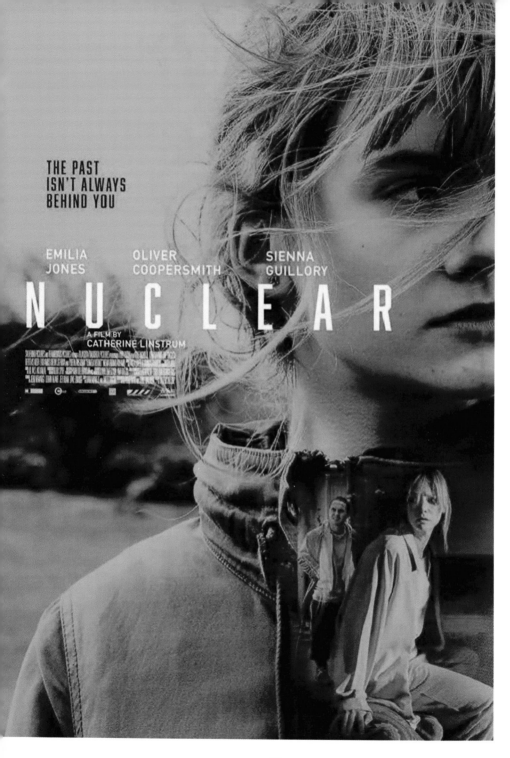

THE PAST
ISN'T ALWAYS
BEHIND YOU

EMILIA   OLIVER   SIENNA
JONES   COOPERSMITH   GUILLORY

NUCLEAR

A FILM BY
CATHERINE LINSTRUM

The Big Tower of Darkness: Haunting Energy in Catherine Linstrum's *Nuclear*

Helena Bacon

Susan Owens suggests that 'Ghosts [move], as ever, with the times.'[1] Written by David J. Newman and directed by Catherine Linstrum, *Nuclear* (2020) depicts a thoroughly modern haunting through blending a gothic narrative of family trauma with a broader tale of nuclear sites, histories and energies. Imre Szeman and Dominic Boyer suggest that '[t]o be modern is to depend on the capacities and abilities generated by energy.'[2] The looming presence of the decommissioned Trawsfynydd nuclear power station, an imposing landmark in its Snowdonian setting, and the secrets it contains are connected by uncanny and charged means to narratives of recent nuclear disaster – namely Fukushima – and its lasting effects, and to more domestic horrors in Linstrum's production. *Nuclear* sees 14-year-old Emma witness her brother savagely beating their mother in secluded woodland; Emma rescues her and drives to an empty guest house in mid-Wales where the pair rest and hide. Emma befriends a local boy and they break into the power station, looking for a way to incorporate it into his base-jumping hobby. Her mother meanwhile is haunted by a Japanese ghost who we later find out is a spirit created by the Fukushima disaster; she has come to guide the mother's spirit over to the afterlife and out of the Welsh limbo she is trapped in. Meanwhile, Emma's brother locates her and eventually reveals that he, too, is dead (Emma had stabbed him when he killed their mother) and his ghost sinks into one of Trawsfynydd's containment ponds. Emma sees her mother's spirit one last time before she departs.

The film echoes Gabrielle Hecht's assertion that 'going nuclear', from splitting and fusing atoms through to the adoption of nuclear energies and the creation of nuclear weapons, creates ruptures in nature's very building blocks, just as ruptures appear in Emma's family, and in her perception of time and reality.[3] Atomic forces here, however, are also presented as agents of resolution, and at the film's end are connected explicitly to a kind of 'righting' and reclamation that complicates Peter Bradshaw's reading of them in the film as 'malign energies'.[4] Hecht suggests that 'asserting the ontological distinctiveness of "the nuclear" [carries] political, cultural and economic stakes, amplified by morality talk'; this assertion tends 'to boil down to a simple duality: nuclear technology [represents] either salvation or depravity.'[5] Linstrum's film suggests that all things nuclear exist as both of these extremes *and* within the spaces in between them. The nuclear here is a force that both creates and mends tragedy, and as a material and immaterial presence: both a square, grey power station spoiling the landscape, and an international psychopomp, or certainly, in Linstrum's film, a spirit very far from home, borne from Fukushima to Snowdonia by strange nuclear forces. By fusing a domestic haunting with international nuclear narratives, *Nuclear* creates a kind of nuclear gothic that appears to reinforce reading the nuclear as either side of a binary presentation, but actually, upon further inspection, complicates and conflates these two disparate possibilities.

Trawsfynydd itself is an unusual scar on the British landscape, and indeed the British nuclear landscape. It is a Magnox station, meaning it has no outer containment buildings and is gas-cooled, and its twin reactors are housed in the conjoined towers the film depicts against the greenery of mid-Wales. It has not operated since 1991, when it was closed on safety grounds. Almost 500 jobs were lost and a review of this ruling by Nuclear Electric in October 2011 found the station was still not fit to generate power – the station did not produce enough revenue to cover modifications, and the welded joints in its pressure vessels were receiving high doses of neutron radiation from the reactor cores which embrittled the steel and risked them cracking.[6] The cores were jeopardising the structures built to contain them safely (just as Emma's brother has not been safely 'contained' and placated through his position in the family). It is thought that decommissioning Trawsfynydd will take around 100 years. Andrew Smith states that the 'Gothic […] mutates across historical, national, and generic boundaries as it reworks images drawn from different ages and places.'[7] Trawsfynydd is presented by Linstrum as a specifically modern Gothic ruin, complete with dark towers, dripping tunnels, and green-lit storage pools, that emphasises the human vulnerability of Emma and the boy when they break in, and still poses a risk to them and to its environs because of the site's lingering radioactivity.

Smith suggests that 'the uncanny, whilst a psychoanalytical concept, can also be used to bring to light historically contextualised anxieties'.[8] The uncanny here is deployed both as a means of working through familial violence but also to address anxieties concerning nuclear techno-sciences and what the human has done with the nuclear. Trawsfynydd is connected through haunting to the Fukushima disaster of March 2011, that took place only months before the Welsh power station was once again declared unsafe. The Tohoku earthquake caused a 46-foot-high tsunami that then hit the Daiichi nuclear plant and destroyed much of the site. Three reactor cores melted, and four reactors were written off. *Nuclear's* ghost from Fukushima, discussing the end of her life, states in the film's opening that 'when it happened, it happened very fast. My family is gone, and I am gone too. It's very difficult when you die so quickly. It makes you lost for a very long time.'[9] After articulating both her absence and the reason for her presence in Snowdonia, she then benignly haunts Emma's mother, who is either also dead or clinging to the last moments of life while her spirit in turn haunts the Welsh cottage. The Japanese ghost keeps her within the safe confines of the retreat and its immediate vicinity, appearing in a variety of colourful outfits and warning the mother against getting close to the power station in search of Emma. She describes at the film's close how '[t]he big tower of darkness came, and it took away my home and my family. It was so quick that I had not time to understand what was happening'; her situation is similar to the way Emma's mother has been murdered quickly and unexpectedly, though in different circumstances.[10] We might presume that the 'big tower' she mentions is the giant wave but her speech is sufficiently ambiguous as to also generate images of the atomic bombs dropped on Hiroshima and Nagasaki in 1945, the first and only atomic weapons dropped deliberately on civilian environments. Joseph Masco states that 'the detonation of the first atomic bomb marked the end of one kind of time, and the apotheosis of another, an uncanny modernity that continually exceeds the language of "national security", "mutually assured destruction", the "Cold War", or even "terror".'[11]

This uncanny and transgressive modernity is made manifest here with a ghost that is a product of one nuclear disaster and an apparent echo of another, a palimpsestuous spirit who overlaps different strands of Japan's nuclear history (and, connectively, America's) and a British nuclear site and issue also. The general passing of time, and the moments and incidents that punctuate and interrupt it, are merged with specific nations and spaces and the temporally static properties of haunting. This suggests that nuclear energy and its ability or preponderance to linger means it can and does cross spatio-temporal boundaries. This 'haunting' is also evidenced in ongoing nuclear properties and processes. Robert Macfarlane suggests that '[w]e know how to make electricity from uranium and we know how to make death from it, but we still do not know how best to dispose of it when its work for us is done.'[12] The half-life of uranium-235 is around 700 million years. It decays very slowly, and this breakdown can directly kill living cells or cause alterations to DNA. Radiological contamination can also taint surfaces and substances, similar to the ways in which the gothic mode can appear in or alter other genres and forms, the mutations Smith outlines.

These lingering presences (radioactivity and the ghost it has created) have this effect on the family drama Linstrum presents. When Emma first explores the Trawsfynydd area, after she and her mother alight there, she sees the boy standing on a bridge – presumably by the Llyn Trawsfynydd reservoir. She later says to him 'I thought you were a ghost.'[13] Indeed, the film never confirms the reality of the boy, nor denies it – he is never named, and we don't see him interacting with anyone but

Emma throughout the narrative. We see nobody but the people Emma interacts with and the Fukushima ghost, the suggestion being that the boy might be one more spectre seemingly conjured by or in the orbit of the power station, which draws Emma and her attendant ghosts to it in a form of human and spatial fusion. The boy also mentions a friend we never see, Anton, from the Ukraine, another possible indication of a haunting – he is never depicted and provides a further link to broader nuclear histories. When they are exploring the power station, the boy claims that 'this place, it was used for weapons in the Cold War', and says that '[i]n the Cold War, me and Anton would be enemies, but now we go nuclear together.'[14] He also mentions Chernobyl, saying to Emma that it is now full of wolves.

Despite the fact that Trawsfynydd did not directly help to generate nuclear weapons – Magnox reactors were designed to produce both electrical power and plutonium for the British nuclear weapons programme – Chernobyl did affect Wales and its nuclear culture and environment. Seán Aeron Martin and Mari Elin Wiliam state that 'radioactive dust from the accident penetrated the uplands of North-west Wales', causing agricultural disruption – the radioactive cloud hit much of the country but North Wales in particular was prone to it settling and permeating the ground due to specific environmental conditions.[15] Furthermore, 'the catastrophe was harnessed by more conventional nuclear agitators to highlight the dangers of producing nuclear energy.'[16] Campaigners questioned the 'radiation's ownership: did it really all stem from Chernobyl or was there more sinister "domestic" radiation at work, particularly emanating from Trawsfynydd.'[17] The film echoes and responds to the cultural enmeshment and international contamination and transference, as occurred in 1986, in the narratives and incidents it stitches together – 1945, 1986, 2011, 2020 – and in the way it presents haunting and spectral connections: the ghosts here can and do move across borders (both national and material) and make connections beyond those normally established in more typical, static or spatially limited hauntings.

Although the Fukushima spirit does tell the mother's ghost that certain places are off-limits – 'this place is not for you', she says to her when she tries to cross the reservoir bridge towards the power station – spirits here are still granted far more freedom to blow across land and border than 'standard' hauntings, and they settle in the Welsh landscape in a kind of inverse of the Chernobyl disaster: they don't emanate (seemingly) from the plant but are instead drawn to it (the boy is not Welsh so has also seemingly come from elsewhere). They embody some of the concerns of the 1980s nuclear campaigners in designating Trawsfynydd a possibly dangerous presence in the landscape. This would explain in part why there is no one present in Trawsfynydd or the surrounding area in the film, and how easily Emma and the boy break into the station (they only cut one lock, and no one stops them).

A decommissioned power station would still be staffed and guarded, so either the film is using artistic license in its presentation of the station as a 'real' ruin or is framing it as a kind of phantasmagorical beacon that calls in spirits and those involved in their passing.

The film also reflects smaller aspects of nuclear processes in its more intimate, domestic narrative. Macfarlane states that 'sometimes we bury materials in order that they may be preserved for the future. Sometimes we bury materials in order to preserve the future from them. Some kinds of burial aspire to repetition and reinheritance (storage); others aspire to oblivion (disposal).'[18] Macfarlane is discussing both burials generally and the Onkalo nuclear waste storage site in Finland specifically. Spent nuclear fuel and contaminated radiological tools and materials must be either buried or submerged in water in spent fuel ponds. Emma, in her relationships with her mother and her brother, engages in the two types of storage Macfarlane outlines. She, we work out at the film's end, has left both semi-buried in secluded woodland after her brother killed her mother and Emma killed him, after years of him abusing them both. Not realising her mother has died, or in a form of denial or misconception facilitated by the company of her mother's spirit, Emma preserves her mother in a kind of buried isolation in both the woodland and at the retreat in order to protect her, to make sure she carries on 'repeating' in Emma's life. She both kills and leaves her brother in order to protect her mother and herself, and the wider world, from his sadistic and volatile behaviour going forward. She repeats this burying again when his spirit traces her position and she pushes him into one of the fuel-storage ponds at the power station. This submersion marks the start of Emma's recovery from the limbo she has found herself in: rescuing her brother – bringing him back into the present – and risking her own health by diving in to the pool herself, means that his spirit is forced to acknowledge his own volatility and culpability.

Anna Storm states that '[t]he physical and mental landscapes scarred by radioactivity, by political conflict, and by fear are intertwined with preconceptions of the possibility to clean up, to control, and to exert responsibility.'[19] Building on this sense of possibility, Hecht states that '[g]lobal warming, Western fears about the impact of the alleged 'clash of civilizations' on the world's oil supply … and Bush's bedroom relationship with the 'nuclear' industry are combining to transform nuclear power from ecological Satan to planetary saviour.'[20] Though not Emma's 'saviour' explicitly, Trawsfynydd and its nuclear properties and interiors – lit with uranium-green strip-lights that give the interior a stereotypically nuclear hue – does become the locus of the realisation that her immediate family are dead and that she has killed her own brother. His ghost, however, when she has pulled it from the radioactive storage pond, says to Emma 'You hurt me so much. It had to be done.' Though his language seems at first accusatory, by saying that she needed to hurt him to end him, he absolves her from all wrongdoing and takes responsibility for his own actions before he sinks back into the pool.[21] Emma's submersion in the nuclear pond, while dangerous (the boy finds her and washes her to mitigate the water's harmful effects), acts conversely as a kind of cleanse.

Nuclear properties are also here implicitly contrasted with other fuels and energies: when her brother finds Emma in the retreat, he douses her in what she thinks is petrol (it is really water) and shouts 'I am the fire.' While emphasising his instability and cruelty, it also connects to traditional, more obviously polluting forms of energy – oils and coal, fossil fuels that are burnt to generate power. The brother's malignant energy is aligned with these older fuels, contradicting associations we might still retain regarding the 'unstable' nature of nuclear energy – his anger and hurt, which have seeped in violent ways into Emma and her mother's lives, are framed as akin to these older pollutants rather than the atomic forces harnessed at the plant. The nuclear washes him away – it provides a further 'clean up', a means for him to accept responsibility and to dissipate having done so. While the film overlays nuclear energy with hauntings, destruction and distortion, it also depicts Trawsfynydd and its nuclear ambiance as, if not liberator, then at least site and engine of their resolution.

Owens suggests that a '[g]host's capacity to be about things other than themselves is being recognised more fully now than ever'.[22] *Nuclear* presents individual, historical and structural modern hauntings, networking both ongoing ambivalence towards nuclear power with the ambivalence we can normally locate in the gothic mode. It literally and metaphorically accounts for the dangerous aspects of nuclear power by presenting Trawsfynydd as a 21st-century ruin (which is, essentially, what it has been) and tracing its presence and properties back to international nuclear disasters that have lasting and ghostly effects, but also obfuscates this reading by making this Welsh nuclear plant and its environs a form of safe haven for Emma and the ghost of her mother, and 'providing', through its energies and histories, a kind of spectro-historical grid which generates a guide who helps Emma's mother move into 'the next place'. This ambiguity, presented through both the real nuclear site and imagined nuclear hauntings, acknowledges nuclear power's dangers without exorcising all possibility that it might also provide a future for us, that even radioactive decay might (eventually) contribute to the creation of the future. Indeed, as of 2020, Trawsfynydd is set to house a new research facility, developing new approaches to low carbon power, nuclear energy and medical technologies that just might resolve some of the lingering negative effects of previous nuclear disasters and placate their attendant ghosts.[23]

. . . .

Helena Bacon

Notes

1. Susan Owens, *The Ghost: A Cultural History* (Tate, 2017), 203.
2. Imre Szeman and Dominic Boyer, *Energy Humanities* (John Hopkins University Press, 2017), 1.
3. Gabrielle Hecht, 'Nuclear Ontologies' in *Energy Humanities*, 250.
4. Peter Bradshaw, 'Nuclear review – escape to the post-apocalyptic country' in the *Guardian* (5 November 2020), https://www.theguardian.com/film/2020/nov/05/nuclear-review-catherine-linstrum-emilia-jones-sienna-guillory (accessed 15 March 2021).
5. Gabrielle Hecht, 'Nuclear Ontologies', 250.
6. Tom Wilkie, 'Safety fears lead to nuclear plant closure' in the *Independent* (23 October 2011), https://www.independent.co.uk/news/uk/safety-fears-lead-nuclear-plant-closure-welsh-power-station-first-be-shut-down -because-possible-danger-1486111.html (accessed 15 March 2021).
7. Andrew Smith, *Gothic Literature* (Edinburgh University Press, 2007), 4.
8. Smith, *Gothic Literature*, 15.
9. Catherine Linstrum, dir., *Nuclear* (2020, Snowdonia, BFI/Ffilm Cymru Wales/S4C), DCP.
10. Linstrum, *Nuclear*.
11. Joseph Masco, *The Nuclear Borderlands* (Princeton University Press, 2006), 1.
12. Robert MacFarlane, *Underland* (Hamish Hamilton, 2019), 399.
13. Linstrum, *Nuclear*.
14. *Ibid*.
15. Seán Aeron Martin and Mari Elin Wiliam, 'Politicising Chernobyl: Wales and Nuclear Power During the 1980s', *Transactions of the Royal Historical Society*, vol. 29 (2019), 273-92.
16. Martin and Wiliam, 'Politicising Chernobyl', 275.
17. Martin and Wiliam, 'Politicising Chernobyl', 276.
18. MacFarlane, *Underland*, 409.
19. Anna Storm, *Post-Industrial Landscape Scars* (Palgrave, 2014), 47.
20. Hecht, 'Nuclear Ontologies', 250.
21. Linstrum, *Nuclear*.
22. Owens, *The Ghost*, 263.
23. Allan George, 'Unlocking the nuclear potential of Trawsfynydd' in *North Wales Chronicle* (30 September 2020), https://www.northwaleschronicle.co.uk/news/18760021.unlocking-nuclear-potential-trawsfynydd/ (accessed 15 March 2021).

Amos

Samantha Mayne

Amos had been an employee of All-You-Mart for thirty-two years, eight months and nineteen days when he was called into the small room at the back of the storage dock.

His commencement date was emblazoned in tiny white print on his bright blue employee identity tag. Beneath that was a QR code that served to reassure All-You-Mart that he was wherever he needed to be, whenever he should be there. Amos always was. The Rorschachesque clouds of black and white that made up the code reminded Amos of a pair of opposing swans, long and broken-looking necks curving toward one another to form the shape of a pixelated heart.

The room was quiet and empty, save for a featureless wooden desk and a black chair on the opposite side. The leather on the back had worn away to a tired-looking grey in a wide patch the approximate size and shape of a man's torso. He had been here before. Several times. The Floor Manager's office was the room they had been brought to when he had been taken on by All-You-Mart under the Post-war Reemployment Scheme. His whole division had been taken to the same megastore, thirty-two ex artillery operators. He had overheard the manager at the time – Amos didn't know if he'd ever learned his name – saying that it was easier to keep the divisions together.

"Build on existing dynamics: war and retail aren't all that different."

Amos was able to understand that. His role at All-You-Mart felt like a minor deviation from his military duties. Take the products from the big metal cart. Locate the tag for the product on the shelf. Place the product. *Load, Aim, Fire.*

The other ex-military employees were gone now, of course. For what little it still sold, All-You-Mart did not need thirty-two stock replenishment staff. They barely needed Amos.

The coffee disappeared first, about two years after Amos had started working at the store. Bananas, then chocolate. Avocados and peanuts, about ten years in. The milk and honey had stopped in the same week, just a few years ago. Some of the customers and staff had found that amusing. Amos hadn't known why. The most recent loss was the fish, eight months ago.

The fish had made Amos sad. He'd never been to the ocean – at least, he didn't think he had. He might have been stationed near the coast during the war, but that time had become an indistinct miasma of red skies, thick smoke and graveyard silences fractured by ballistic eulogies. When Amos tried to remember the war, it was like peering through the smoked glass window in the manager's office. Vague shapes, grey murmurs of movement that might have been anything. The only distinct memory he had from that time was the

Prime Minister's announcement when the war had ended. The middle-aged man telling soldiers and citizens alike that the fight was over, that their soldiers would remain Useful in this new world of peace and prosperity. His clear voice, thin and sharp as it broke the formless drizzle of the war. A bolt of lighting in the rain.

When he wasn't busy, before the store opened for the day or after it had been closed, he would go and look at the mackerel and sea bass arranged neatly on the faux grass that lined the seafood fridges. He would peer into their glassy, unseeing eyes and imagine them swimming in the great, blue everywhere of the Atlantic. He'd wondered if fish knew they were in the Atlantic. Or the Pacific. Or the Arctic before the Arctic had become a place where no fish could live, before it had turned from everywhere-blue to nowhere-black. Once he had stared so long at the unblinking eye of a red emperor that the store opened around him without his notice. The Floor Manager had to ping his company receiver, over and over, until the man had simply come and thumped Amos on the back. Told him that if he stopped working like that again he'd be out of a job.

The Floor Manager did not like Amos, and more than once had stated that he was too old to be working the floor, out around The Customers. Amos knew he was old, older by far than anyone else at the store, but he liked to be near The Customers. He liked The Customers and the noise they made and the mess The Customers left behind on the slowly emptying shelves. He liked to show The Customers where to find the vitamins and the dried beans and the water filters and the prophylactics and the rice flour and the sedatives and the motor oil. And more than anything, when he had finished helping them, Amos liked to ask The Customers; "Have I Been Useful To You Today?" and they could tell him Yes or No or any number of answers in between and their answer would be reported to management and most days Amos got more Yes's than No's, and that made him very happy.

Amos was thinking of his Yes's and No's while he waited in the Floor Managers office. He was quite sure he had plenty of Yes's, and not a single No so far today. Amos had been Useful. So surely, he had thought, he was not here because he was in trouble. The last time he had been to the office, he was in quite a lot of trouble. There had been a complaint. From a Customer. The first one Amos had ever received. He hoped that he had not been complained about again. Last time, he had been sent to retraining for a month, and when he returned, all the fish were gone.

The last complaint had come from the mother of two small boys. Amos shouldn't have known that, but the Floor Manager had told him when he had called Amos into the office.

"A mother of two and a Class Six Citizen, Amos! Do you know how many Sixes still shop here?"

The boys had been watching Amos place boxes of sunscreen on a shelf. *Load. Aim. Fire.* The smaller of the two had approached, straining to reach a thin tube of SPF 150 from the highest shelf. His fingers brushed the smooth plastic and knocked several bottles onto the ground. The boy had looked bashful. He had a striped green towel over his shoulder. Messy white-blonde hair. A tooth missing, right at the front.

Amos had picked up the fallen sunscreen and handed a tube to the boy. The boy took it and grinned. The gap in his tooth exposed a tongue that was stained an artificial ice-lolly blue. Amos asked the boy if he had been Useful to him today.

He didn't hear his reply. Amos would never know if the boy had been a Yes or a No. A cold stream of water had hit him and pulled his attention to the second child. Taller. Wider. Holding a bright yellow gun as long as his arm, a bulbous chamber protruding from the top. The word *Toy* did not thunder across his brain like a wave of mortars and cut-off screams. The word *Weapon* did. *Weapon* and *Danger* and *Protocol* and *Load. Aim. Fire, Load. Aim. Fire, LoadAimFIRE.*

A security drone had captured the incident, and when Amos had been hauled into the back the Floor Manager had shared the footage.

Amos thought that surely it could not be him, throwing his bulk between the small gap-toothed boy and the larger one who brandished the sun-coloured water pistol. Sending the small one flying into the shelf, plastic tubes of lotion clattering to the ground and aping the hollow *rat-tat-tat* of spent machine gun cartridges. The figure that had dropped to one knee and held the weightless ghost of a blast cannon, pulled from a distant dream, was an imposter. The Amos-like thing that mimed *Load. Aim. Fire* in the direction of the now crying older child, that ignored the shouting of The Customers and the staff who had rushed over to pull the dazed smaller boy from the wreckage of the sunscreen shelf was a mirage, an illusion, a nonsensical scribble over the logic that guided Amos's identity. Amos was not a soldier. Amos was not loud and deadly and necessary. Amos stocked shelves at an All-You-Mart. Amos was quiet and good and Useful.

The Floor Manager had wanted to be rid of him after that. He had called Head Office, in front of Amos, and said as much. The faceless, static-tinged voice on the other end of the call had transformed the Floor Manager's face into a rictus of distaste and impatience. He had not shared with Amos what Head Office had told him. Just spat the word "Retraining" in his direction before leaving the room.

Amos could hear voices heading towards the Floor Manager's office, and he hoped he was not being sent to retraining once more. It was not that it had been bad, per say. It just hadn't been much of anything. Without the changing faces of The Customers; the banners and signs that transformed from Happy Christmas to Happy Easter to Happy Halloween and back again; the slowly depleting cans and cartons on the long white shelves, he found each day, each hour, melded into the next. He barely remembered a moment of it. What he did remember was his first day back at the store, returning with anticipation to the seafood case and finding nothing.

Nothing was not correct. The too-green faux grass was still there. The translucent, knobbly plastic beneath the grass that was supposed to look like ice but looked more like shards of broken glass was still there. There was even something new, a little sign that read:

All-You-Mart regrets to announce that fresh fish is no longer available in stores. For citizens class four and above, please contact Head Office for alternative options.

But there were no fish. No glimmering silver scales, or bulging eyes filled with frozen ocean. Just pretend grass on pretend ice, an apology, and Amos's own reflection staring back at him, a spectre trapped beneath the glass.

The door to the office opened, and the Floor Manager entered with a woman Amos had not seen before. She wore a grey coverall, carried a black bag and did not acknowledge him. The Floor Manager sat in his chair. Stared across the desk at Amos.

"We don't need you anymore."

He did not tell Amos why. Why or why *now*. Amos did not ask either. Instead, he asked:

"Are there no more fish left in the ocean? Are they all gone now? Like the coffee? Like the bananas?"

The woman in the coverall was standing behind him. She made a surprised sound. The Floor Manager was typing something into his computer. He did not look at Amos again.

"There haven't been fish in the ocean for a long time. They were from a pond, in a shed in Victoria. Shed's closed now. Pond went bad."

The woman snorted at the Floor Manager.

"You talk to your vacuum cleaner like that too? They should never have given these things voices. Makes everyone sentimental, start treating them like people. They aren't."

With that, the woman behind Amos took a thin silver rod from her square black bag and jammed it into the back of his neck.

The device that had been running on a declassified-for-the-commercial-market version of the Australasian Military Operating System – AMOS – had been returned to basic functionality.

Amos could no longer remember the war, or All-You-Mart, the fish or the gap-toothed boy with the sunscreen. What was left behind in the repurposed combat bot was enough to have him stand and walk into the back of the van that waited to take him to landfill.

It was enough to have him tramp over the mounds of microwaves and plastic bottles, the single, abandoned shoes and burnt-out automobiles. The sun-faded, unwanted toys and discarded air filtration masks. The things that once had meaning. Form. Things that no longer did. There was enough left for him to lay down, unassisted on the tallest pile of refuse and to stare up at the empty sky.

As his shutdown screen began to overlay his external visual feed, the sky seemed to change from a dull, weathered grey to the great, promising and impossible everything-blue of the ocean, and as the final, fleeting sparks of awareness flickered and died in the spaces between his metallic synapses, there was enough left for Amos to hope.

And he hoped that he had been Useful.

. . . .

Samantha Mayne

UNIVERSITY OF CHICHESTER

Be Inspired,
Be Original,
Be You

Become an author with one of the UK's leading MA in Creative Writing programmes

Visiting Professors include award-winning novelist Kate Mosse and Man Booker Prize nominee Alison MacLeod. Tutors include Suzanne Joinson, author of *The Photographer's Wife* and *A Lady Cyclist's Guide to Kashgar,* and Naomi Foyle, author of *The Gaia Chronicles*. Recent graduates include authors Glenn Brown (*Ironopolis,* Parthian Books), Juliet West (*The Faithful*, Pan Macmillan) and Graham Minnett (*Anything for Her*, Zafre).

We also run MAs in English Literature, Cultural History, The History of Africa and the African Diaspora. **Closing date for applications is 1st August 2020.**

Contact Professor Hugo Frey, Head of Humanities, for more information:
Email: H.Frey@chi.ac.uk | **chi.ac.uk/ma-creative-writing**

'Hansel and Gretel',
Otto Kubel.

Recipe for a Fairy Tale

Elizabeth Hopkinson

There are many variations on this timeless recipe, which dates back to the oral tradition. The hazelnuts give a lovely, old-fashioned flavour, although many people nowadays prefer a fairy godmother.

1 apple, poisoned on one side, harmless on the other
1 enormous turnip
3 bowls of porridge
As much gingerbread as you can eat
6 golden goose eggs
1 pea (dried)
5 beans (magic)
3 hazelnuts (optional)

Select a suitable oven. An iron stove works best, but always inspect first, to ensure it is not occupied by an entrapped prince seeking your hand in marriage.

Pre-heat the oven to its maximum setting. Take great care when testing the temperature so as not to fall in. If in doubt, trick a witch into doing it for you. This has the added benefit of ridding you of the witch if you succeed in pushing her in. In this case, take extra care not to burn down the house.

Place the pea under twenty mattresses and twenty feather beds. This does nothing to enhance the flavour, but is useful in testing the veracity of any would-be princesses who come calling.

Open the hazelnuts and remove dresses of gold and silver, each more beautiful than the last. Wear dresses on successive nights to attend the palace ball. Take care to leave before midnight.

Mix dry ingredients in a bowl. A magic porridge pot is ideal, as it will multiply the ingredients to the required amount. Safety warning: always have an agreed password to halt multiplication, as pots of this sort have a tendency to fill the entire neighbourhood.

Dice the apple and turnip and add to the mixture. Again, take great care with sharp implements. Limbs, and even heads, have been known to grow back, but there is no guarantee.

Whisk the eggs to a light, fluffy consistency. On no account let yourself be tempted to cut open the goose that laid them. It's not made of gold, and you won't have any more eggs.

Add remaining ingredients and stir vigorously, with assistance from talking animals and helpful strangers.

Grease and line an ovenproof tin. Use plenty of elbow grease. This will either come naturally, since your family treat you as a domestic servant, or be a great challenge, as this is the first time you've done a decent day's work in your life.

Bake the mixture until you smell the blood of an Englishman.

Remove from oven and allow to cool. Keep a close eye on it, in case it becomes sentient and runs as fast as it can.

Serve with a side of last-minute revelations and tearful reunions.

The beauty of this recipe is that it can be stretched to serve any number, although 3, 7 or 12 is traditional. If you do find you have leftovers, these can be baked into a humble pie and served to your former tormentors.

. . . .

Elizabeth Hopkinson

Kai at 37

Jon Stone

after The Snow Queen

The silver thread that snuck into my eye
has grown into a blot, a second pupil.
The other mirror-spike has swollen too,
I'm sure – a solder splash across the heart.

What can you do but learn to love again?
This sorcery being so well inscribed,
with such a marked effect, it seems unlikely
that any tear will burn the stain away.

I'll smile, then, at each flared, caruncled face,
bite down upon these skewered scorpions.
I'll bear the blood-soaked sun, the flooded town,
and kiss the ash that was my sister's hair.

I'll learn to love as well my own poor frame,
the sickly-skinny moving mulch of me.
In time, I dare say I'll even come round
to treasuring these bitter silver coins.

. . . .

Jon Stone

Shibata Zeshin,
'Kuebiko'.

Kuebiko

Jon Stone

Picture the prince of scarecrows stood in his field
on a mountain above the world, pert as a general,
nothing left unsurveilled and all of it logged.

Steady through theatre of rain and snowy applause.
Impervious to lit torch and locust alike –
stalwart of stalwarts. Watchman for every season.

But just suppose that you've heard it wrong. Suppose
it's the seeing itself that roots him, and not upright
but flat on a bed, concussed with the implications.

Suppose that the knowledge of even a fraction of what
is taking place would knock any sound mind sideways –
the way it all matters but doesn't, is plotted but isn't.

And Kuebiko, propped on one splintery arm, leans out
from a torrent of visions to unwrap a salient fact,
but longs for a story, a lie, or a lazy judgement.

"The spell to cast off is a spell for one eye clouded,"
he says, as he tips his pipe out into the ocean.
And somewhere beyond you both, a door flies open.

. . . .

Jon Stone

Note
Kuebiko is the Shinto kami (deity) of knowledge and agriculture, represented in Japanese mythology as
a scarecrow who cannot walk but has comprehensive awareness.

'Frog and Mouse' by Getsuju, a Japanese artist of the Edo period.

Frog

Jon Stone

after Chrono Trigger

The rain summons from its ranks
this one glum knight, belly-chinned,
in armour nippled and puckered with rust.

A survivor of the *Froschmäusekrieg*,
fled into lake or trench when Slice-snatcher
made bloodied guac of his brethren.

Or else: an erstwhile river-stone, sublimed
into a pikeman by Nikushi (the Frog Lord),
his weapon broken on a buckler.

Either way, he's living debris. A little joke,
tucking his grab-bag collection of bones
inside a muddied, iridescent cape.

Unless, of course, he's the prince brought low,
brought to ruin – now a bloated old soak
bent to the tap of night's heavy, hoppy ale.

Or, as he seems momentarily, entirely to be
in the moon-sized blasts of the headlamps,
a stout skeleton, grown into his frogskin,

not the storm's squire but its sorcerer.
Steadfast as a sign in the road,
courteous before you, his unmaker.

. . . .

Jon Stone

Note
Chrono Trigger is a 1995 Japanese role-playing game released on the SNES/Super Famicom, in which
Frog features as a playable character.

Carl Blechen, 'Stormy sea
with Lighthouse', c.1826.

Black Lullaby

Christie Maurer

The drunk sea thrashes
the black-toothed cliff side, eternal
child pitching a fit, it gathers its flowing
skirts once more to throw itself
on daggers. I know people like this, tireless,
who favour the floor's backhand
to their glued-together shatterings.
I feel a splintering, the metallics
of blood in my mouth, hair-line crack
at my heel, precious fault
snaking up the leg again. I hang my skin
on the tree's blue limb and sit in the sand.
It blows and snaps – a sheet set to dry.
Exquisite – veins twist
red over blue – tapestry.
I stare unflinchingly, lidless,
at the high windows the wind whistles.
My forgotten sister lives there,
combing her hair, gliding room to room.
Her lily-long fingers touch
every small object. She's waited,
patient for a visit. Like a needle,
the seascape pierces
her eyes and fills her with longing
for its glass edge, while the sea spreads
its waters searching for something to hold.

. . . .

Christie Maurer

'What did she find there but real ripe strawberries'.
Arthur Rackham's illustration to the Brothers Grimm,
'The three little men in the wood' (1917).

Winter Strawberries, a Song for Unwanted Children

Christie Maurer

1.

There, on her lips, the taste for it.
She imagines her mouth
           on the tip of something sweet.

    Mother made me
        in twilight with a man
    who rinsed her body
and held it on his tongue like cake.

    Her body is
          white communion.

Let snow bathe us! Let us imagine
       our mouths on the tip of something sweet.

2.

All morning at the window, she sits.
The back of her head framed by hoarfrost.

I imagine her eyes, dark and searching
for something she wants under the snow.

With eyes deepened from staring, mother turns back at me.
As if I were an illness, she studies me.

The fire crackles in its sooty pit.
I hear her latch the door from outside.

3.

Strawberries don't grow in winter, I know

                but mother made me
                        this paper dress, said *go*

    fetch me a basket of strawberries.

    By the fire she sits, counting her flames,
    like the gold coins she keeps in her purse.

    I lie in her great hand like a coin to be spent.

Something in us that will lie in a hand.
    Something in a heart is glad to kill.
    Something sweet.

4.

None of them invite
             me inside beside
                    their fires
though they can
          see my feet
               are turning blue,
see my breath
          freeze and fall
               like my paper dress
will. Soon,
      I am naked.
          So what,
let them stare.
        I will break
            all their windows.

5.

Into a whiteness that obliterates, I enter
the mind laid bare.

I will spare you my hunger, my handfuls of snow.

6.

> Mother bathes in milk and drinks wine
> my hands make a cup, my mouth is dry
>
> waiting for someone to love me.

7.

When I found myself I found a cove of melting snow
and within the cove a briar, densely knotted

thick with thorn, and within the briar
a patch of kindness: wild strawberries –

startling, red, dripping, wet,

like the Christ Child inside the flaming heart.

8.

In the eaves the swallows sing sweetly
a song for children lost in the woods.

I imagine my mouth. Mother
in a bath of lit coals—

I imagine cruel mothers in us all.

. . . .

Christie Maurer

A review of

By the Fire: Sami Folktales and Legends

Victoria Leslie

The stories collected by the Danish artist and ethnographer Emilie Demant Hatt during her time living among the nomadic Sami in Swedish Sápmi are revived in this new English publication by Barbara Sjoholm. Originally published in 1922, *By the Fire: Sami Folktales and Legends* was the culmination of summers spent with the Talma and the Kareesuando Sami, following the tented communities or *siidas* as they followed the annual reindeer migration and chronicling the tales told to her 'by the fire'. This new edition not only includes Demant Hatt's original black-and-white linoleum prints and her field notes but also includes a useful Afterword by Sjoholm. This addendum sheds light on Demant Hatt's advocacy for Sami culture, her transformation from a seasonal tourist to a self-taught ethnographer – studying the Northern Sami language at the University of Copenhagen in the process – and ultimately her approach to 'ethnography through immersive living'.

It is this approach which granted her so much time in the company of Sami women while the men were away managing the reindeer herds, and which Sjoholm identifies as separating her from her male contemporaries who were preoccupied with folktale typology and privileging the perspectives of male storytellers. In comparison, the majority of the stories in *By the Fire* are told by women, often emphasising a female point of view. For Sjoholm, Demant Hatt's focus on women's lives was due to the fact she was a venturous 'New Woman', advancing into male territory as both an independent traveller and ethnographer.

By the Fire begins with a series of aetiological tales: 'The Sami Who Weren't Satisfied with the Moose' explain how the reindeer came to be the preferred animal of the Sami, while 'How the Sami Were Given Reindeer and Tents by the Underground Folk and How the Settlers Were Given Farms and Farm Animals' explain how a union between the Sami and the underground folk gifted the Sami with the tools of their livelihood (their reindeer, tents, lasso and skis). Other tales similarly tell of Sami men entering exogamous marriages, particularly with the daughters of the cannibalistic ogre, Stallo, who is invariably outwitted by the newlyweds after attempting to cause them trouble. In these stories, young, otherworldly brides often represent wealth and prosperity, whereas older women frequently feature in the collection to represent hardship and adversity. In one tale, an old woman is credited for chasing the reindeer away and thus making herding difficult, while in another, an old woman is responsible for unleashing mosquitoes into the world after tiring of their incessant buzzing while carrying them in a sack on her back.

Though a vast proportion of the stories included in *By the Fire* feature encounters with fantastical foes, stories about mortal enemies, of Scandinavian settlers and Russian *Chudes* (bands of thieves) coveting Sami resources reveal how a history of persecution has found its way into oral tradition. Some of these tales depict the Sami outsmarting their adversaries by, for instance, singeing the hair off a prized reindeer to prevent it from being stolen, or by taking refuge in a cave only to re-emerge three hundred years later when the coast is well and truly clear. However, other stories, such as 'When the Farmers Wanted to Stamp Out the Sami' and 'The Headland of the Murdered' reveal genocidal ambitions directed at the Sami. As Sjoholm relates, together with a long record of Sami rights being systematically eroded and Sami lands appropriated by private landowners and state authorities, the Sami have no word for war. What they have instead is a repertoire of stories about resistance and resilience.

This is particularly evident in the tale 'The Sami Girls Who Escaped the Bandits' in which a Sami girl is kidnapped and detained via her braids. Forced to share a bed with her captors, the sexual threat implicit, she waits for them to fall asleep before cutting off her plaits and escaping into the wilderness, picking her way across a bog that ultimately leads to her pursuers' demise and her survival. The moral of tales of this kind, which sometimes feature a pair of scissors instead of a knife, reasserts the importance of being prepared and necessarily equipped for potential danger. The importance of the knife and the axe in earlier tales in the collection, where the touch of metal has the capacity to control or vanquish otherworldly entities, also adheres to European superstition that iron can repel or contain supernatural forces and adds double weight to their significance in Sami culture.

Whether the stories in *By the Fire* speak of encounters with fantastical entities or people with subhuman motivations, they champion Sami resilience and heroism in the face of adversity and provide a welcome introduction into the world of Sami storytelling. Furthermore, Sjoholm's Afterword provides contextual insight to the stories and the storytellers who Demant Hatt interviewed, fundamentally highlighting the richness of Sami storytelling culture and the work of a much-overlooked pioneer in Scandinavian folklore collecting.

Collector/illustrator: Emilie Demant Hatt. Translator: Barbara Sjoholm.
Publisher: University of Minnesota Press (2019), 208pp.

. . . .

Victoria Leslie

A review of

Fantasies of Time and Death: Dunsany, Eddison, Tolkien

Joseph Young

ritic Brian Attebery has written of the 'new coherence'[1] that Tolkien's *The Lord of the Rings* provided to the modern fantasy genre, claiming it provided a model against which future essays in the craft can be and are judged. This is a credible point. In her new book, however, Anna Vaninskaya observes a key thematic carry-over between Tolkien's legendarium and those of two critically neglected authors who beat him into print by healthy margins. 'Cosmogony and eschatology,' she writes in her introduction, 'how it all began and how it is all going to end, and the nature of mortal existence in the interim between creation and apocalypse, is ultimately what the fantasies of Dunsany, Eddison and Tolkien are all about.' (6) The introduction furthers the point by briefly observing this theme in three more pre-Tolkienian fantasists (William Morris, George MacDonald and Hope Mirrlees). Vaninskaya does a convincing job of observing a strong thematic coherence in the pre-Tolkienian genre, positioning Tolkien as less of an innovator than a particularly robust link in a chain.

Having said this, Vaninskaya begins what may be her weakest chapter, that on Lord Dunsany. She observes that Dunsany's preference for short forms produced a corpus of discrete examinations of a few key motifs rather than (as in Tolkien) a single continuous thesis on them. That is a relevant point, though Vaninskaya seemingly does little to organise these individual thematic sorties into a rhetorical campaign. She identifies five such motifs – the extinction of humanity, gods in exile *et al.* – as dominating Dunsany's *Fifty-One Tales*. The reader might expect a subchapter on how Dunsany develops each of these motifs across his oeuvre. What follows instead is an elongated discussion of Dunsany's influences and precursors on the theme (Swinburne, Shakespeare, Tennyson). *The Gods of Pegana* and *Time and the Gods* are briefly examined, though only as the chapter progresses does any concerted focus on how Dunsany instantiates Vaniskaya's theme really emerge. Of his works only *The King of Elf-Land's Daughter*, *The Blessing of Pan* and *The Charwoman's Shadow* are given sustained individual attention, resolving into cohesive case studies of the putative subject matter. All, it is worth noting, are among Dunsany's full-length novels. Of Dunsany's aggregate oeuvre, Vaninskaya concedes she can make few solid conclusions (59). Whether her theme is best handled in larger literary works, or her methodology works best in relation to such texts, is an interesting question.

Whichever of these two points is cause and whichever is effect, the later chapters of the book are considerably more successful in drawing conclusions about Eddison and Tolkien, who both did their best work in longer forms. If Vaninskaya's decision to treat Eddison's Zimiamvia trilogy as a unit is mildly frustrating (all her page references are to the 1992 omnibus edition), her focus on this work is commendable and the results are well-informed and intriguing. The key marker of strong Eddisonian criticism, I think, is the ability to see his ornate prose style as a part of his heartfelt polemical message, rather than as a barrier thereto. L. Sprague de Camp, in his woefully misapprehended 1976 profile,[2] failed in this; Jon Garrad, in his 2015 comparison of 'ERE' to modernism,[3] succeeded, and got some fine work done as a result. Vaninskaya should be bracketed with Garrad. Her work on such matters as Eddison's use of bubbles as a visual and compositional motif, his repeated yet subtle references to Rupert's drops (toughened glass beads created by dripping molten glass into cold water) and his discussion of Vandermast's House of Peace – one of several devices he uses to telescope or compress time – are impressive, and all are presented convincingly as instances of the core theme. Her observation that the central tension of Eddison's trilogy is epistemological rather than ontological – that this is a story about two interrelated groups of characters *working things out* – is particularly strong. The chapter has the same overall feel that its subject text, read carefully, has; it is a solid, cohesive examination of an important, undersubscribed subject.

Things continue to improve in the final chapter, which presents the tension between the human and Elvish perception of time as Tolkien's key authorial concern. This is hardly innovative, though Vaninskaya handles the issue very well. She hits upon the key matter of why themes of time and death loom so large in fantasies of artistic ambition fairly early in her composition; 'the tragedy of being a man' – which Tolkien identifies in '*Beowulf*: The Monsters and the Critics' – 'necessitated as its foil the tragedy of being an Elf' (156). Fantasy can do things other prose literature cannot, among them presenting points of contrast to the human condition. Vaninskaya observes that Tolkien essentially reverses the intuitive implications of mortality and immortality; his Elves, being eternally linked to their world, lack the freedom to make something of themselves – and their world – that his Men have. This is an interesting insight and one on which she expands at some length in the copious remainder of her chapter. The end result is less of an impassive discussion of a theme than a celebration of it and the authors and literature that concern themselves with it.

Indeed – and at the risk of contravening C.S. Lewis ('We don't need the critics to enjoy Chaucer, we need Chaucer to enjoy the critics') – it could be said that the key strength of this book is that it leaves the reader keen to revisit all three subject authors and reconsider their works in light of the author's numerous interesting points. Vaninskaya's work on Dunsany may be the least good material here but it is by no means poor, and the Eddison and Tolkien chapters are highly commendable. This is an important study of two critically undersubscribed authors and an impressive look at a third who benefits from reconsideration in relation to them. It is not the last word on any of its subject texts, but it serves as a robust contribution to a weighty, potentially inexhaustible debate.

Author: Anna Vaninskaya.

Publisher: Palgrave Macmillan (2020), 272pp.

. . . .

Joseph Young

Notes

1. Brian Attebery, *Strategies of Fantasy* (Indianapolis: Indiana UP, 1992), 14.
2. L. Sprague de Camp, *Literary Swordsmen and Sorcerers* (Sauk City, WI: Arkham House, 1976).
3. Jon Garrad, 'The Conquerer Worm; Eddison, Modernism and the War to End all Wars', in Janet Brennan Croft (ed.), *Baptism of Fire: The Birth of the Modern British Fantastic in World War I* (Altadena, CA: Mythopoeic Press, 2015).

Hans Christian Andersen in Russia

A review of

Hans Christian Andersen in Russia

B.C. Kennedy

I n the summer of 1857 – the same year as his translation of 'The Emperor's New Clothes' – Leo Tolstoy undertook a European tour. His travel reading included Hans Christian Andersen's *The Improvisatore* but it was Andersen's fairy tales that Tolstoy admired, writing in his diary, 'Andersen is excellent' (124). This anecdote illuminates the longstanding canonical status Andersen has for his Russian readers, but this status is owed specifically to his fairy tales; an assertion that the multinational scholars involved in this collected volume make in their introduction. For nearly two centuries, they argue,

Andersen's fairy tales have become 'an organic part of the cultural memory of generations of readers, his texts constituting a particular cultural code that is actualized in various artistic fields'.

The volume is divided into three parts, beginning with 'Andersen and Russia in His Time', focusing on how Russia was conceptualised by Andersen and by Danish culture at large. Mads Sohl Jessen demonstrates how Andersen's view of Russia changed from a negative one to an avid appreciation of Russian literature from the 1830s onwards. Johs. Nørregaard Frandsen emphasises the crucial role played by Denmark's Princess Dagmar's marriage to the future Emperor Alexander III (1866) in forging stronger Danish-Russian cultural bonds at a time when Russia was beginning to be integrated into Western European capitalism. Certainly, by the 1890s Andersen had become a universally recognised classic in Russia: in 1894 Peter Emanuel Hansen and his wife, Anna, translated Andersen's fairy tales and selected other writings, which became the canonical Russian translation of the Danish storyteller in the 20th century, through the Soviet period and beyond.

The second and third parts of this volume demonstrate the overarching chronological framework from the earliest Russian references to Andersen in the 1840s to his pervasive presence in the Russian digital sphere of today. Part Two, 'Andersen in Russia's Cultural Contexts', is divided into three subsections, with the first examining Andersen's place in pre-revolutionary Russian literature and criticism. Inna Sergienko's paper demonstrates that a positive re-evaluation of Andersen's works from the 1880s onwards changed the initial critical response. This was, she argues, due to the increasing availability of suitable translations and changing attitudes toward the fairy tale as a genre. Ben Hellman's investigation of the relationship between three major Russian writers of the 19th century and Andersen concludes this section.

In '"Creative Affinities": Andersen in Silver Age Poetry and Prose', the extraordinary influence Andersen played for a number of major Russian Silver Age poets is addressed. Oleg Lekmanov demonstrates how Acmeists such as Anna Akhmatova, Osip Mandelstam and Nikolai Gumilev were primarily interested in the material world of Andersen's stories of animated toy figures and preoccupied with deeply imaginative readings of Andersen. This was in sharp contrast to the younger Symbolist writers who were captivated by how the 'deceptive simplicity of Andersen's tales masked the mystical, almost ineffable Mystery of childhood and childlike purity' (138).

While Karin Grezl offers readers a compelling narrative of how the poet Maria Tsevetaeva modelled aspects of her life and the imaginative landscape of her poetry after Andersen, Peter Alberg Jensen traces the presence of 'The Snow Queen' in Boris Pasternak's *Doctor Zhivago*, arguing that the fairy tale contributes a paradigmatic and symbolic key to the novel.

In 'Andersen's Transformational Legacy in the Soviet Union', Vladimir Orlov explores Stravinsky's and Prokofiev's use of Andersen's fairy tales to express their own aesthetic visions. This is followed by Boris Wolfson's study of the playwright and author Evgeny Schwartz, who adapted three of Andersen's tales into successful plays for children. Wolfson highlights Schwartz's radical innovative departure from the original tales and argues that Schwartz's dramatic versions possessed a 'cultural authority that rivalled, if not supplanted, the popularity of the Andersen texts' in a time of Stalinist repression and persecution (246). Marina Balina addresses the 'thaw'[2] in Soviet cultural life and how the writer Konstantin Georgievich Paustovsky uses Andersen's fairy tales as an emblem of imaginative freedom (256). Ilya Kukulin's essay of late Soviet culture provides an engaging discussion of numerous artists and writers in the 1950s, '60s and '70s who used Andersen's stories as a foundation for formulating new artistic visions.

In Part III Helena Goscilo's comparison of 20th-century film adaptions of the Danish 'Little Mermaid' to the Russian *rusalka* unwittingly emphasises a problematic element in Andersen's text, namely the sexualised imagery of the little mermaid and her sisters. Yuri Leving focuses on how artists sought to distance themselves from official Soviet socialist-realist doctrine. In his view, Andersen's importance to Russian illustrators lies in 'the liberating vision his tales afforded their art form' (116). Andrei Rogatchevski argues that 'The Snow Queen' resonates particularly in Russian due to the 'mirroring of Russia's self-identification with the North' (16). Helena Goscilo's second contribution assesses Soviet and post-soviet Russian graphic art inspired by 'The Little Mermaid', while the final collaborative essay analyses how Andersen's fairy tales permeate the commercial, digital and primary-educational culture of present-day Russia.

Given the preponderance of Russian fairy and folk tales such as those of Alexander Afanasyev, the popularity and enduring legacy of Andersen's fairy tales is not fully explained in this collection, but it does explore how the perception of Russian 'Anderseniana' – the extensive and multi-stranded legacy specifically of Andersen's fairy tales – functions in Russian cultural memory. However, what is precisely meant by a cultural code that emerges from Anderseniana is not made clear in this book. There are some editorial issues present but they are minor, and overall, this is a fascinating and wide-ranging read for those interested in why Andersen remains one of the top three authors in demand in Russia today.

Editors: Mads Sohl Jessen, Marina Balina, Ben Hellman and Johs. Nørregaard Frandsen.

Publisher: University Press of Southern Denmark (2020), 480 pp.

. . . .

B.C. Kennedy

Notes

1. The Silver Age of Russian poetry is an artistic period that dates from the very late 19th century and ends in the 1920s. It implies a wide range of poets, genres and literary styles. There is even a broader notion of the Silver Age of Russian culture that includes avant-garde art, theatre, cinema, photography and sculpture – which very frequently were created in artistic groups that consisted of people from different spheres.

2. The liberalisation that commenced in Soviet Russia the year of Stalin's death is referred to as 'the Thaw'.

A review of

Inviting Interruptions: Wonder Tales in the Twenty-First Century

Apolline Weibel

C ontemporary wonder tales 'invite us to exchange the well-trodden paths of fairy-tale forests for threads of connection across webs of wonder', Cristina Bacchilega and Jennifer Orme declare in the introduction of *Inviting Interruptions: Wonder Tales in the Twenty-First Century* (x). With this intriguing collection of textual, textural and pictural narratives, Bacchilega and Orme question the shapeshifting nature of the fairy tale through the prism of its many transformations across the 21st century. As disturbing and disorienting as this collection might at times be, the editors never abandon you to fend for yourself in search of meaning among the thorns. Instead, with a weaver's precision and light touch, Bacchilega and Orme spin their own, implicit narrative throughout this collection, redefining not only the purpose and shape of wonder, but also its ambivalent relationship with the inviting Other.

Perhaps the most original and inviting aspect of this collection is its constant interweaving of artistic mediums and narrative voices that echo and interrupt one another, sometimes even within a single narrative. The heroine of Rosario Ferré's 'A Poisoned Tale', for instance, comments on the narrative as it is still developing, assessing that the 'story is getting better; it's funnier by the minute' while also remarking that the narrator 'doesn't sympathise with' her (136). The chorus of wondrous voices gathered in this anthology is itself repeatedly interrupted by the editors' own insights and interrogations, forcing us to stop and ponder over these tales, leaving us suspended between the familiar and the unknown, like the boulder overhanging the cottage in Shaun Tan's 'Shelter' (133). Besides, in spite of its meandering structure, Bacchilega and Orme's collection is undoubtedly centred on several themes, including the exploration of queer desires, the fascination for the monstrous, and the cyclicity of abuse and revenge. These themes are woven together into a coherent – if occasionally bewildering – fairy-tale tapestry that might well have been spun from the silk of Shary Boyle's spider-woman sculpture itself (10).

Far from diverting our attention from traditional fairy-tale themes and tropes, the hybrid nature of this collection is always inherently inviting, and the unexpected ruptures in rhythm, style and medium only interrupt us long enough to draw attention to the importance of redefining the wonder tale in light of its contemporary metamorphoses. Thus, in addition to using multiple or unreliable narrators, this anthology disrupts such prototypical elements as sequential storytelling (as with Maya Kern's achronological 'How to Be a Mermaid'), authoritative language and syntax (through the atypical narrative style of Emma Donoghue's 'The Tale of the Cottage') and even the concept of story itself, by blurring the border between tale and object with Su Blackwell's book sculpture 'Once Upon a Time'. By turning the message into matter, and infusing the matter with message, the artists featured in this collection invite in a plurality and hybridity of voices, shapes and agendas within the genre, both intra- and extradiegetically. This way, Bacchilega and Orme remind us that the wonder tale is, above all, made to be interrupted, altered, transformed. After all, as the protagonist of Diriye Osman's 'Fairytales for Lost Children' states: 'The God of Imagination lived in fairytales. And the best fairytales made you fall in love' (85).

Osman's tale also hints at the political power of wonder tales when the protagonist declares that, for his militant pre-school teacher, 'even Story Time was political' (85). With *Inviting Interruptions*, Bacchilega and Orme set out to prove that they are: by deliberately shaping this collection to be as intersectional and inclusive as possible, they invite traditionally alienated voices, crafts and perspectives into the realm of wonder, welcoming Otherness back into the fairy-tale genre. 'The invitations and interruptions these new tales offer ... invite us to imagine the world, not only the world of wonder and marvels but the world around us every day, differently. They invite us to see ourselves differently, interrupt complacency, and imagine Otherness,' they thus declare in the introduction (xiii). Without having to sugarcoat its tales or shy away from the darkness and horror intrinsic to the genre, this anthology urges us to sympathise with monsters like Maya Kern's carnivorous mermaid and Shary Boyle's aptly named 'Beast' (55), as well as to make space for neurodivergent and disabled protagonists like the heroines of Kelly Link's 'Swans' and Donoghue's 'The Tale of the Cottage'. Similarly, we are encouraged to support and engage with contemporary attempts at queering and decolonising traditional tales and myths, and even to envision potential transbiological and post-human worlds with works such as Tan's futuristic and intriguing 'Birth of Commerce' (47).

With this original and hybrid collection of wonder tales, Bacchilega and Orme extend to us an invitation to wander – and get temporarily lost – in the woods of contemporary folklore and fairy tales. While the constant shifts in format, culture, tone and medium can often prove a little disorienting, they also draw attention to the porous borders of the genre and the many missing perspectives and silenced voices it has become urgent to reclaim and celebrate. Thus, instead of merely observing the transformation of the genre throughout the 21st century, we are forced by the numerous deliberate interruptions contained within this anthology – be they commentaries, questions, or even unclickable video links – to become active participants and truly engage with the material. As readers and spectators, we must therefore seek out missing information, imagine the elements that cannot translate to the page (such as shape and texture), piece together morsels of biased information and draw our own conclusions from them. Indeed, only by inviting ourselves into these tales and accepting to interrupt and modify them can we, in turn, hope to recognise and reclaim our own of sense of otherness and wonder.

Editors: Cristina Bacchilega and Jennifer Orme.
Publisher: Wayne State University Press (2021), 254pp.

. . . .

Apolline Weibel

A review of
Staging Fairyland: Folklore, Children's Entertainment, and Nineteenth-Century Pantomime

Jonathan Roper

In this work, Jennifer Schacker, whose earlier book *National Dreams* (2003) dealt with 19th-century fairy tale collections, turns her attention to the links between fairy tales and pantomime. And as much as it is a discussion of pantomime, this book is also (or maybe more) an intervention into debates in fairy-tale and folklore studies.

The work consists of five chapters, together with a substantial introduction and an 'afterpiece'. These mostly, though not entirely, concentrate on the Victorian pantomime, though there is some discussion of the pre-Victorian pantomime. Pantomime's continuing 20th- and 21st-century life is beyond the purview of the work. Schacker's central argument is that the fact that many Victorians would have known fairy tales in the form of pantomime has been overlooked by fairy-tale scholars, who have instead concentrated on the print and oral circulation of such stories. She discusses her goals in the following terms:

> tracing nineteenth century repertoires across media and in relation to pantomime performance requires a reconfiguration of our thinking about fairy tales – their bearing on questions of identity and sociability, genre and ideology, and also their signifying possibilities. (22)

To give an example of the overlooking of stage fairy tales, she brings up the case of one Victorian writer on *Little Red Riding Hood* who sees Perrault-derived versions as the tale's form in England. However, as Schacker rightly points out:

> by 1878, Red Riding Hood was firmly entrenched as a stock pantomime character, and the story with which she was associated was a stock pantomime plot … this kind of 'Red Riding Hood' could well be considered another 'English version of the story' – very well known and widespread (189-90)

Her chapters and sub-chapters cover a variety of cases. Perhaps the most interesting of her sub-chapters is the one that discusses the work of Thomas Crofton Croker, where she presents the intriguing case of 'Daniel O' Rourke'. In his *Fairy Legends and Traditions of the South of Ireland* (1825), Croker claimed that a man of this name was one of his informants. Speaking against this is the fact that a character called 'Daniel O'Rourke' had appeared earlier in both a tale in verse and in a play. (Another detail that Schacker martials to attack Croker's account is that he would have only been 15 at the time, but I am not sure that this is necessarily a problem: an intelligent 15-year-old could certainly record a tale). Croker, with Walter Scott's encouragement, subsequently transformed the story into a pantomime, which in turn was published. As Schacker notes, it certainly is

> striking that one source for the story that is never mentioned in the footnotes [to the book of the pantomime] is that of a face-to-face encounter between Croker and his 'good friend' Daniel O'Rourke on that June day in 1813. That is understood to be a fictional conceit, one that requires no further discussion (100)

In short, what has been hailed as the first field collection in these islands now seems much less securely so. Perhaps Robert Hunt's 1828 fieldwork then takes the laurels.

On the whole, the case the author makes is fair. Yet, as may happen in books with a thesis, a fair case can be overstated and its supposed adversaries mischaracterised. To give an example, we find on page 108 that W.J. Thoms' work is characterised as 'Francophobic'. Is the author of 'Lays and Legends of France' (1834) a Francophobe? The man who speaks of 'the natural vivacity by which the French are animated'? The style may be overripe, but the sentiment is not Francophobic. There are similarly dubious claims (144) about Thoms' 'virtual erasure' of many popular literary texts. Thoms was interested in popular print (what he called 'English Folk-Books'), and his very first publication was an edition of *Early English Prose Romances*. The bibliography reveals that this treatment of Thoms is based on the reading of a grand total of four pages from his output.

Richard Dorson, despite being (or perhaps because he is) the key figure in the establishment of academic folklore studies in the USA, has become something of a *bête noire* in that discipline in recent years, and is another who comes in for harsh words. It does seem remarkable that a great deal of attention is given to condemning past scholars, whereas contemporary scholars do not receive the same amount of scrutiny. Such a situation is unlikely to pertain in, say, history or sociology, to give just two examples of other disciplines. Nor was it the case in American folklore studies of the 1970s. I am not sure that it is a heathy state of affairs when a discipline spends more time in debate with dead scholars than with living ones.

Overall, there are remarkably few factual errors or imprecisions in the work. The Captain Swing riots began in east Kent, but were not confined there (29). The Charles Dickens writing in 1896 is Charles Dickens jr (176). The author negotiates her way through the minefield of when to use 'English' or 'British', and 'Great Britain' or 'the United Kingdom' (in its 19th-century extent) almost entirely unscathed.

As said at the start, this work is really an intervention in fairy tale studies disguised as a book about pantomime. It has interest when taken on these terms. It will also be of benefit if it brings international attention to the pantomime and underlines the links in the life of fairy tales between stage and page. For me, however, the work's main merit is the wonderful set of more than 27 pantomime images its pages are illustrated with.

Author: Jennifer Schacker.

Publisher: Wayne State University Press (2018), 296pp.

. . . .

Jonathan Roper

A review of

Merpeople: A Human History

Victoria Leslie

When Animal Planet's docufiction *Mermaids: The New Evidence* was aired back in 2013, the American National Oceanic and Atmospheric Association received so many enquiries from credulous viewers that it had to release an official statement denying the existence of mermaids. Despite the network's disclaimer that the programme was entirely fictional, the combination of computer graphics and interviews with actors duped viewers into believing. Likening the programme to the furore surrounding P.T. Barnum's famous 19th-century fraud, the 'Feejee Mermaid', Vaughan Scribner considers in his new book, *Merpeople: A Human History*, our perpetual fascination with the fabled sea folk and our readiness to believe in their existence.

Scribner provides numerous examples of our unwavering belief in the existence of merpeople in his comprehensive study spanning the last thousand years: from 16th-century cartographers peopling the seas of the New World with mermaids, to Benjamin Franklin's candid reportage in the *Pennsylvania Gazette* of a 'Sea Monster' just off the coast of Bermuda in 1736. 'Mer-mania' reached such a peak in the early 19th century that a mermaid sighting, specimen or show appeared in printed media at least once a month. This eagerness to believe was often stoked by unscrupulous purveyors of 'mermaid' specimens, showmen like P.T. Barnum or the sea captain Samuel Barrett Eades, who passed off Japanese-crafted forgeries as the real thing. Though the likes of Barnum and Eades capitalised on the public's credulity, they tapped into what Scribner highlights as the driving force behind his book, our insatiable preoccupation with subaqueous realms and their inhabitants.

As Animal Planet's docufiction suggests, our own era is no less obsessed with these denizens of the deep. But while earlier periods exaggerated the monstrous female power of the mermaid – her image furnished medieval churches, for instance, as warnings to the laity about female lust – the 20th century sees the mermaid swim into more commercial and consumerist channels. The subject of advertisements and films, the modern mermaid is the poster girl of commodity culture, selling everything from coffee and tuna to movies and theme parks. On the silver screen, the mermaid of mid-20th-century blockbusters *Miranda* (1948) and *Mr Peabody and the Mermaid* (1948) conforms to the femme fatale archetype, seducing married men and luring them away from domestic safety. In all of these representations, sex sells, with the mermaid unable to shield herself from the objectifying gaze of those eager to behold and possess her.

The fact Scribner's research focuses so heavily on the female form of the mermaid is explained as the product and legacy of the Christian Church's concerted effort in medieval times to 'dethrone femininity'. Depicting salacious and sexually overt representations of mermaids, including the two-tailed mermaid parting her tails to expose her genital area, religious leaders sought to destabilise female power while highlighting the virtues of piety and self-denial. But the history of merpeople is not just the story of objectification, exploitation and consumerism. As Scribner asserts, in more recent times the mermaid and her kin have moved into new channels, reflecting changing ideologies and evolving understandings of identity and gender, with mermaids and tritons elected as symbols of feminism, body positivity and LGBTQ+ rights.

It is also in more recent times that scholarly work about merpeople has proliferated. This constitutes part of Scribner's own research and prompts the question, what it is about *Merpeople* that makes it unique? Drawing on monster theory, Scribner explains that his study of merpeople, in the words of historian Erica Fudge, is enacted through the process of 'reading through humans'. The examination of aquatic folk in this way sheds light upon the 'ever-changing, often-contradictory ebbs and flows of the human condition'. Though Scribner succeeds in charting the impact and influence of merpeople on human history, why humankind is perpetually looking toward the water is more slippery. Nevertheless, *Merpeople* is a rich and rewarding read and a comprehensive and engaging addition to the merfolk corpus.

Author: Vaughn Scribner.

Publisher: Reaktion Books (2020), 320pp.

. . . .

Victoria Leslie

A review of

The Arts of Angela Carter: A Cabinet of Curiosities

B.C. Kennedy

The catalyst for this book was the exhibition 'Strange Worlds: The Vision of Angela Carter' that Marie Mulvey-Roberts co-curated at the Royal West of England Academy in Bristol in 2017 to celebrate the life, work and multi-disciplinary interests of the iconic late 20th-century feminist writer Angela Carter (1940-92) 25 years after her death. This is the continuation of a tradition triggered by the first edited collection by Lorna Sage in 1994, published after Carter's death in 1992, and the anticipated Bloomsbury publication due to be published in 2022.

In the Introduction Mulvey-Roberts explains that although Carter is generally regarded as a London writer, she wrote more than half her novels while living in Bristol, and it seemed appropriate, therefore, to draw attention to Carter's neglected links with Bristol. The contributors – including leading Carter scholars – focus on the diversity of her interests and versatility across different fields. This book foregrounds Carter's multidisciplinary interests and influences, which allows each chapter to function as part of a cabinet of curiosities and each author 'invites' the reader of this collection into a Carteresque curious room.

In the opening chapter, Michelle Ryan-Sautour explains how the breadth and variety of Carter's short fiction demonstrates the far-reaching intertextual and intermedial diversity of her writing, providing 'powerful, multimedial spaces of fictional reflection for her reader'. This is followed by Anna Kèrchy's exploration of Carterian poetics of space from the vantage point of a 'feminist psychogeographer' who challenges generic conventions and gender roles. Concerned with deconstructing misogynistic images of women, Kèrchy is drawn to Carter's short stories with place-based titles such as 'The Bloody House', recognising that Carter's fiction has been distinguished by a topography of the carnivalesque with such liminal settings as Bluebeard's Gothic castle, Uncle Philip's rundown magic toyshop and Colonel Kearney's travelling circus.

Julie Sauvage revisits Carter's short stories by focusing on the complex interplay between painting and music in *The Bloody Chamber*, showing how Carter creates literary hybrids, while

Sarah Gamble's chapter on Carter's poetry – situated in the context of British poetry in the mid-1960s – reminds us that this is a neglected aspect of Carter's work that predates her fiction.

Another often overlooked aspect of Carter are the translations she made from French, which provided an important stimulus for her imagination and creativity. Martine Hennard Dutheil de la Rochère points out that this laid the groundwork for translating and adapting Charles Perrault's fairy tales in *The Bloody Chamber and Other Stories*, while *Black Venus* revisits Jeanne Duval's cycle of poems from a female perspective.

One of Carter's lesser-known interests is anthropology, and Heidi Yeandle suggests that the work of Claude Lèvi-Strauss played a central role in Carterian fiction through her portrayal of supposedly primitive communities in *Heroes and Villains* and *The Infernal Desire Machines of Doctor Hoffman*. The extent of Carter's interest in religion, on the other hand, has often been underestimated, which is hardly surprising since she was a self-proclaimed atheist. In the following chapter Mulvey-Roberts examines Carter's critiques of Judeo-Christianity and its influence on Western cultural myths that hold oppressive gender roles in place. In addition to discussing how Carter demythologises religion, this chapter makes the first extensive interpretation of an episode from *The Passion of New Eve* in relation to Zero and his exploited female followers, based on real-life American cult leader Charles Manson. Through this fictionalisation, Mulvey-Roberts argues that 'Carter not only reveals the potential harmfulness of the quasi-religious messianic ideology fuelling certain cults, but also exposes the burgeoning disillusionment with the Summer of Love'. Catherine Spooner also invokes the counter-culture of the 1960s through her discussion of Carter's short essay, 'Notes for a Theory of Sixties Style' (1967), which presents a condensed account of some of the major sartorial concerns of Carterian fiction throughout her career. This chapter explores the ways in which subculture style became a major influence on Carter's aesthetic sensibility.

Gina Wisker explores how Carter rewrites the constraining myths for women, maintaining that her writing was crucial for the later 20th-century rebirth of Gothic horror. This chapter traces how Carter unpicks the fascination which Edgar Allen Poe and H.P. Lovecraft had with the mythologising of women as monstrous, vulnerable and enthralling. Helen Snaith looks at the power dynamics relating to gender and performance within the puppetry and performance of Japanese culture which fascinated Carter. Alongside a reading of 'The Executioner's Beautiful Daughter' and 'The Loves of Lady Purple', this chapter argues that Carter deliberately uses images employed with *bunraku* (a form of traditional Japanese puppet theatre) in order to challenge the dichotomous relationship between the puppet and the puppet master. Snaith suggests that by using theatrical tropes within both tales, Carter challenges authority within an overtly phallocentric society. Carter's puppets must 'still ultimately adhere to a performance that is imitative of gendered and socio-political expectations in Japan'.

Caleb Sivyer reconsiders Angela Carter's relationship to cinema, arguing that it is important to acknowledge that she was much more ambivalent about this medium than is often noted by scholars. The chapter plays on this ambivalence and suggests that *The Passion of New Eve* and *The Infernal Desire Machines of Doctor Hoffman* employ cinematic-inspired techniques from classic Hollywood films in order to increase the sense of proximity between spectator and spectacle. In the final chapter Maggie Tonkin examines how Carterian writing has often been read through the prism of theatricality, focusing on the representations of literal performance in her work.

As this book demonstrates, place and space were important to Carter, producing an extraordinary vitality in her intermedial work which continues to be relevant today. Representing the transgressive, subversive and iconoclastic, this collection of essays may be seen as a building block that continues to be revisited in the newly emerging discipline of Carter studies. Erudite, cross-referenced and meticulously footnoted throughout, this is a compelling read.

Editor: Marie Mulvey-Roberts.

Publisher: Manchester University Press (2019), 275pp.

· ·

B.C. Kennedy

A review of

101 Middle Eastern Tales and Their Impact on Western Oral Tradition

D.L. Ashliman

A widespread legend tells of a man who dreams of treasure in a distant town, but upon going there he discovers that the treasure is actually at the place he has left and on his own property. Those familiar with English folklore know this story as 'The Pedlar of Swaffham', first recorded in Abraham de la Pryme's diary (10 November 1699) as a 'constant tradition'. Here the leading character is directed by a dream to go to London, where he shall hear 'joyful news'. Once in London, the pedlar is belittled by a man for having foolishly followed a dream. The Londoner himself had dreamed of a treasure buried under a particular tree in the village of Swaffham, but was not foolish enough to have pursued it. The pedlar realises that the tree thus described is on his own property, returns at once to his home village, and digs up the treasure.

This legend, always with essentially the same plot, has been localised in dozens European cities and towns, where it typically claims to be the record of an actual event, not a make-believe fairy tale. In spite of its broad European distribution, this story was not born in the West, but rather in the Arabic-speaking Middle East. Its earliest recorded version is found in the anthology *Deliverance Follows Adversity*, written in Iraq in the 10th century by al-Muhassin ibn Ali al-Tanukhi. Here the leading character is a citizen of Baghdad who dreams that a fortune awaits him in Cairo. Arriving there he is ridiculed by an Egyptian who claims that he himself had dreamed of a treasure in Baghdad and relates details about the treasure's location. He concludes that he was not foolish enough to make such a long journey because of a mere dream. Recognising the site revealed in the Egyptian's dream, the man from Baghdad returns home and finds the treasure.

'The Man Who Became Rich through a Dream' is but one of the 101 Middle Eastern narratives identified and analysed by Ulrich Marzolph as having impacted Western oral tradition. His Middle Eastern sources are primarily works originally composed in Arabic, Persian, or Ottoman Turkish. A retired professor of Islamic studies at the Georg-August University in Göttingen, Germany, Marzolph is uniquely qualified to conduct this comparative study of the Muslim world's contributions to European folktales. His forty years of occupation in this field include three decades of editorial involvement with the prestigious 15-volume *Enzyklopädie des Märchens*, where he also has contributed numerous articles on European as well as Middle Eastern oral traditions.

The author opens each of the 101 chapters with a European or New World sample of the relevant story, followed by a discussion of important variants. In the best folkloric tradition, wherever possible he chooses versions recorded directly from oral informants, typically in the 19th or 20th century. Marzolph's design to begin each chapter with an *oral* version of a Western tale ensures that each of the 101 stories represents a tale type that is both timeless and cross-cultural in its appeal. In many instances these stories were heard, told, and retold by the uneducated, even illiterate, segments of society. Their appeal thus responds to basic human concerns, and not necessarily to a sophisticated intellectualism.

In each chapter Marzolph then moves to Middle Eastern precedents of the tale, including the narratives themselves as well as the history of their original composition and subsequent distribution, both orally and in writing. He concludes each chapter with copious notes, which together with the bibliography of works cited (pp. 597-669), containing about 1700 entries, constitute a valuable research tool in their own right.

The organisation of Marzolph's *101 Middle Eastern Tales* follows the Aarne-Thompson-Uther (ATU) type index of international folktales and includes at least one example from each of the major groups (Animal Tales, Tales of Magic, Religious Tales, Tales of the Stupid Ogre, Anecdotes and Jokes, and Formula Tales). Reflecting the type of story most likely to migrate between disparate cultures, the category best represented in Marzolph's book, with 65 samples, are the anecdotes and jokes (ATU types 1200-1999). These stories, often referred to as jocular tales, are typically brief and unsophisticated in their humour, thus lending themselves to easy memorisation and cross-cultural migration.

Many of the stories included in Marzolph's sampling of this category will be quite familiar to Western readers. For example: the fools who try to keep a bird from escaping by building a fence around it (ATU 1213); the foolish man and boy who end up carrying their donkey while trying to please every passer-by as to who should ride on it (ATU 1215); the fool who digs a hole in the ground to dispose of an unwanted pile of dirt (ATU 1255); the fool who fails to count the donkey he is riding (ATU 1288A); and the enchanted tree (ATU 1423 – a tale included both in Boccaccio's *Decameron* and Chaucer's *Canterbury Tales*). As he does throughout the book, Marzolph presents these tales mostly in recently collected oral versions, thus showing them in new light, as does his tracing of their genealogy to their Middle Eastern origins.

101 Middle Eastern Tales can be read on two levels. At its elementary level the book is an anthology of timeless stories, presented both in their original Islamic dress and also in the forms they have developed after migrating to the West. The chapters can be read in any order; each one constitutes an independent unit consisting of two or more reading selections plus an accompanying interpretive essay.

The interpretive essays reveal both the depth and the breadth of Marzolph's scholarship. His unique ability to illuminate parallels as well as distinctions between the cultures of the Middle East and those of Europe as reflected in their oral traditions ensure this book's future as a standard reference tool.

Author: Ulrich Marzolph.
Publisher: Wayne State University Press (2020), 716 pp.

. . . .

D.L. Ashliman

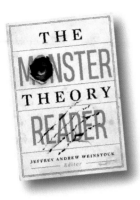

A review of

The Monster Theory Reader

Willem de Blécourt

I n the more than twenty years of its existence, monster studies has generated enough publications to compile a Theory Reader. The big question, however, remains whether studying 'monsters' shines light on them collectively, or even individually. Is 'monster' a useful category? This reader brings together 24 articles, some of which are actually chapters from other books, written by 14 men, 10 women, and one person using 'they/them' pronouns. One of the chapters is co-authored. There are 14 Americans, four inhabitants of England, two Australians, one Japanese roboticist, one French psychoanalyst, as well as another psychoanalyst from Austria. Two of the contributors have passed away. After Jeffrey Jerome Cohen named the field 'monster culture' in the late 1990s, it still bears the signs of its inventor's gender. White male Americans are clearly in the majority; apart from one Japanese contributor and one from London with a South Asian heritage (the last with an American co-author from a similar ethnicity), all contributors are white. The relevance of this becomes clear in the chapter by Annalee Newitz, in which she describes the film *From Hell* (2001; released 2002 in the UK) as 'the first-ever whitesploitation movie' (266), or in Donna Haraway's article on 'inappropriate/d Others'. The preponderance of white authors in this volume also relates to the relevance of monster studies as a (sub-)discipline.

Monster studies developed at the end of the 1990s, although the expression 'monster movies' is much older and most of the authors will have grown up with it. Some of the contributions were written long before they were published in this volume and obviously not with 'monsters' in mind. This is the case with the non-US authors, such as the Japanese roboticist Masahiro Mori, the French author Julia Kristeva, or the Viennese psychoanalyst. Only one of these, Margrit Shildrik, is an exception; she has written *Embodying the Monster*.

The products of this gathering of authors are like a box of goodies, to be savoured one by one, carefully chewed and then spat out so as to not dull one's critical taste buds for the next sample. The reader can then proceed to read whole books and other works by any of these contributors; or even delve into other monster volumes such as Asa Simon Mittman and Peter J. Dendle's *The Ashgate Research Companion to Monsters and the Monstrous*

(2012), which is the source of two contributions in the present volume. Other examples are Marina Levina and Diem-My T. Bui's edited collection *Monster Culture in the 21st Century: A Reader* (2013), or the *Encyclopedia of Literary and Cinematic Monsters* (2014) by the same editor as this volume. I will not review the whole field here but only point to what I see as some basic flaws.

What are monsters anyhow? As I prefer my monsters to be tangible, I looked at the monsters in the *Theory Reader*, as it is advisable to always relate the theory to the practice. The monsters, then, can be described as basilisks, blobs (after a 1958 film of the same title), cyborgs, demons, devils, dragons, ghosts, ghouls, golems, incubi, krakens, manticores, phoenixes, succubi, trolls, vampires, wendigos, werewolves, witches and zombies. Some of these are only briefly mentioned in the introduction. Eleven authors of 12 chapters, however, refer to vampires. They occur most frequently, followed by the devil featuring in 10 chapters, and ghosts in nine. These monsters derive from literature or films, and created in what I have called 'single author' works. There is barely any discussion about local folklore 'monsters' which are more or less traditional, related by multiple narrators and circulating among wide stretches of the population in general. Devils, ghosts, werewolves, and witches belong to the latter category. It implies that even in the case of 'monsters' with a folkloric background, their cinematic of literary manifestations prevail. Vampires, as presented in Bram Stoker's *Dracula* or in cinematic manifestations are another good example; in an alien country, they are far removed from any folkloric origin. Of course, everyone is entitled to their own monsters, but by not looking at folklore, students of film and literature miss the chance to compare individual creations and more common notions, or to trace how they influenced each other.

Take witches for example. Traditionally, neighbours accused them of bewitching their victims with their decrepit bodies. In this *Theory Reader*, however, they are associated with monstrous births; this is based on a 16th-century document which is misleading as the witches appear in a list of 'monsters' with whom 'direct copulation' would caused these births (8), whereas a witch only caused births to go wrong in her role as crone. Nevertheless, a link to the film *The Witches of Eastwick* (1987) is established in which the babies are anything but monstrous, even though their mothers had been impregnated by a devil. In another place witches appear as the denizens of another world. In a subsequent chapter, the witch is a figure of abjection, 'one of whose crimes was that she used corpses for her rites of magic' (215). The last is in a discussion of horror films, which in itself presents the clue to the particular reading of the 'witch' here. The same author, Barbara Creed, however, also cites a mythologist to illustrate that a 'witch' with long fingers and nose can figure as a 'phallic mother', thus evoking the image of the fairy-tale witch. In Jon Stratton's discussion of the film *Night of the Living Dead* (1968), the Haitian witches appear as agents who turn individuals into zombies – again, a highly circumscribed occurrence. The variety of these mostly 'single-authored' witches is also made clear by including a reference to

Shakespeare's *The Tempest*, or to a spawning of a poisonous spider, or a swamp providing a stage for witchcraft.

Noël Carroll writes that werewolves 'violate the categorical distinction between humans and animals' (139). I would argue against this, since 'werewolf' used to be a label to categorise a particular kind of human criminal. The historical werewolf on which my definition is grounded, however, needs to be seen as completely different from the werewolf in 19th- and 20th-century literature or in films. This is another reason to separate the two categories and to consider the present-day 'monster', as confined to contemporary popular culture, as is the case with the witches.

In conclusion, the collected theories in the *Theory Reader* have one purpose, namely theorising a constructed category of 'monsters', and this runs the risk of becoming a self-fulfilling prophesy. The question of whether 'monster' is a useful category can thus not be answered in the affirmative. Monster studies here seem to be reserved mainly for present-day, white, Anglo-Saxon scholars. The inclusion of single contributions on the Japanese *tanuki* and another on much older monstrous races does not dispel this impression but only confuses the issue. While monsters maybe an entertaining subject for students, without information about the viewers or readers in all their diversity (or the lack of it, whatever may be the case), it is hard to conclude anything meaningful about the role of 'monsters' in these cultures in which they operate today. Yet they may be fun on a university course.

Editor: Jeffrey Andrew Weinstock.
Publisher: University of Minnesota Press (2020), 560 pp.

. . . .

Willem de Blécourt

About the contributors

Dr Paul Quinn

Dr Paul Quinn in Senior Lecturer in English Literature at the University of Chichester. He is the Director of the Chichester Centre for Fairy Tales, Fantasy, and Speculative Fiction.

Dr Naomi Foyle

Dr Naomi Foyle is a science fiction novelist, verse dramatist and award-winning poet and essayist. Her cyberchiller *Seoul Survivors*, named by the *Guardian* as 'among the best of recent SF', was followed by *The Gaia Chronicles*, an eco-science fantasy quartet set in a post-fossil fuel Mesopotamia. A non-Muslim Fellow of the Muslim Institute, she is also a Consultant Editor of *Critical Muslim*, and has spoken on Islamic SF at festivals and events including the Bradford Literature Festival and MFest: Festival of Muslim Cultures and Ideas.

Dr Judith Woolf

Judith Woolf is an honorary fellow in the Department of English and Related Literature, University of York. Her main research interests are 20th-century Italian-Jewish writing, particularly in relation to the Holocaust, and narrative patterns in European literature. Her academic publications include *Henry James: The Major Novels* (Cambridge UP, 1991), *The Memory of the Offence: Primo Levi's 'If This is a Man'* (Troubador, 2001), and translations of Natalia Ginzburg, *The Things We Used to Say* (Carcanet, 1997), Primo Levi and Leonardo De Benedetti, *Auschwitz Report* (Verso, 2006) and *Auschwitz Testimonies: 1945–1986* (Polity, 2018), and Primo Levi, *The Last Interview* (Polity, 2018). Her verse translation/ edition of the Old Norse poem *Völuspá, The Spaewife's Prophecy* was published by *Scandinavian-Canadian Studies* in 2017.

Claudia R. Barnett

Claudia R. Barnett is undertaking a Creative Writing PhD at Deakin University, Australia. Her thesis examines Charles Perrault's 17th-century fairy tales as discourses of disciplinary punishment. Recent publications include creative interrogations of Perrault's work in *TEXT* and *South of the Sun: Australian Fairy Tales For The 21st Century*. Claudia is former Editor-in-Chief of the Australian Fairy Tale Society's e-zine. She currently facilitates Shut Up & Write sessions for the Australasian Association of Writing Programs' HDR Hangout group. Claudia holds a postgraduate degree in nursing and a Master of Arts (Writing & Literature).

Dr Michelle Anya Anjirbag

Michelle Anya Anjirbag recently completed a PhD at the University of Cambridge. Her research interests include adaptation of fairy tales and folklore, and cross-period approaches to narrative transmission across cultures and societies. Her work has appeared in *Jeunesse, Adaptation* and *ChLAQ*.

Dr Helena Bacon

Helena Bacon holds a PhD in Creative and Critical Writing from the University of East Anglia. She has forthcoming short fiction in collections published by Spectral Visions Press and Eggbox, has appeared on podcasts related to gothic and horror fiction and has published several academic articles on various aspects of the gothic, ecocriticism and literature and science. Her first novel was longlisted for the 2017 Mslexia unpublished novel prize and she is currently a teaching associate at the University of Nottingham and a visiting research fellow at the UEA. She is working on her first monograph: *Nuclear Gothic: Textual and Cultural Fusions*.

Dr Jon Stone

Jon Stone was born and lives in Derbyshire. He completed a PhD in poetry-videogame hybridity in 2020, and *Dual Wield: The Interplay of Poetry and Videogames* will be published by DeGruyter in 2021. His collection of poetry, *School of Forgery* (Salt, 2012), was a Poetry Book Society Recommendation. He won an Eric Gregory Award in 2012, and the Poetry London Prize in 2014 and 2016. His website is www.gojonstonego.com.

Samantha Mayne

Sam is a morbid speculative fic writer living in Perth, Western Australia and attending the University of Western Australia. She's convinced the world is going to end one way or another and spends most of her time trying to write down exactly how it's going to happen. She will almost certainly be survived by her two cats, the half-eaten, six-month-old tub of hummus in her refrigerator, and Keith Richards.

Christie Maurer

Christie Maurer is a poet residing in Houston, Texas. She earned her MFA in poetry from Virginia Commonwealth University. She is the recipient of the 2016 Thomas B. Gay Graduate Poetry Award, the 2016 Claudia Emerson Scholarship, and the 2013 Carole Weinstein Poetry Fellowship. Her writing has previously appeared in *Blackbird* and *WomenArts Quarterly Journal*. Currently, she is writing an epic poem entitled 'Experimentation', which she hopes to finish soon.

Elizabeth Hopkinson

Elizabeth Hopkinson is the author of *Asexual Fairy Tales and Asexual Myths & Tales* (SilverWood, 2019, 2020). Her short stories have appeared in *The Forgotten & the Fantastical* and *Dancing with Mr Darcy*, along with many other anthologies and magazines. Her story 'A Short History of the Dream Library' won the James White Award. Elizabeth studied English Language & Literature at the University of Leeds. She has appeared at Leeds LGBT+

Literature Festival, Ilkley Literature Festival Fringe and Swanwick Writers' Summer School. She lives in Bradford with her husband, daughter and cat. Elizabeth is a romantic asexual and is committed to asexual representation in fiction. Her website is elizabethhopkinson.uk.

Dr Victoria Leslie

Dr Victoria Leslie is the author of a short story collection, *Skein and Bone* (Undertow Books) and a novel, *Bodies of Water* (Salt Publishing). She has been awarded fellowships for her writing at Hawthornden Castle in Scotland and the Saari Institute in Finland and her fiction has been shortlisted for the World Fantasy Award, the British Fantasy Award and the Shirley Jackson Award. She recently completed a PhD at the University of Chichester exploring folklore and the New Woman.

Dr Joseph Young

Dr Joseph Rex Young is a teacher, researcher of fantasy literature, based in Dunedin, New Zealand. His research interests have led to him observe George R.R. Martin's *A Song of Ice and Fire*, its televisual extrapolation *Game of Thrones*, and the public responses to both with an informed critical eye. The principle result of this work to date is *George R.R. Martin and the Fantasy Form* (New York: Routledge, 2019), in which Dr Young interrogates a number of commonplaces concerning Martin, particularly the notion that his novels subvert or transgress fantasy norms. Much of the impact and success of Martin's tale, Young argues, stems from the author's ability to get fantasy tropes and imperatives working to his advantage rather than accepting them as impositions. Dr Young's other interests include Gothic literature, ekphrasis, the philosophical novel, and neo-Romanticism.

Dr B.C. Kennedy

Barbara Kennedy received her PhD from the University of Sussex where she studied the links between music and healing as described in a wide range of 15th-, 16th- and 17th-century literature. She has lectured at the University of Sussex and the University of Brighton where she has taught a range of courses, with texts from the medieval period to today. Barbara has an interest in Irish folklore and fairy tales, including the political applications of fairy tales in the 19th and early 20th centuries.

Apolline Weibel

Holder of an agrégation in English literature, Apolline Weibel completed a master's course in Comparative Literature at University College London (UCL) in 2015, before beginning a funded PhD in English and American literature at the Université Sorbonne Nouvelle – Paris 3, under the supervision of Professor Isabelle Alfandary. Her research focuses on the representation of maternity and motherhood in contemporary anglophone fairy-tale retellings. She is particularly interested in the archetype of the wicked stepmother and her role within the mother/daughter narrative. She also teaches literature, theatre, and methodology to undergraduate students at the Université Sorbonne Nouvelle – Paris 3.

Prof. Jonathan Roper

Jonathan Roper is Associate Professor at the University of Tartu, Estonia. He is the author of *English Verbal Charms* (Helsinki, 2005), and editor of *Charms and Charming in Europe* (2004), *Charms, Charmers and Charming* (2008), *Alliteration in Culture* (2011), and *Dictionaries as a Source of Folklore Data* (2020). He is on the ISNFR committee on Charms, Charmers and Charming. and serves on the International Advisory Board of the journal *Folklore* and on the Editorial Board of *Commentationes Archivi Traditionum Popularium Estoniae*. He is also a member of the Folklore Fellows.

Prof. D.L. Ashliman

D.L. Ashliman is Professor Emeritus of German at the University of Pittsburgh, and a leading expert on folklore and fairytales. His website, http://www.pitt.edu/~dash/ashliman.html, hosted by the University of Pittsburgh, is one of the most respected scholarly resources for folklore and fairy-tale researchers worldwide. His recent works include *Fairy Lore: A Handbook* (2005), *Folk and Fairy Tales: A Handbook* (2004), and an edited and annotated collection of *Aesop's Fables* (2003). Past publications include the books *Voices from the Past: The Cycle of Life in Indo-European Folktales* (1993, 1995), *Once upon a Time: The Story of European Folktales* (1994), and *A Guide to Folktales in the English Language: Based on the Aarne-Thompson Classification System* (1987), as well as numerous articles and chapters on related subjects. Prof. Ashliman retired from the University of Pittsburgh in 2000, and he currently continues to research folklore and write prolifically from southern Utah.

Willem de Blécourt

Willem de Blécourt is an historical anthropologist specialising in the study of witchcraft, werewolves and fairy tales in Europe from the Late Middle Ages to the 20th century. He is an independent researcher and an Honorary Research Fellow at the Meertens Institute (Amsterdam). He is one of the editors of the Historical Studies in Witchcraft and Magic series (together with Jonathan Barry and Owen Davies). His own books include *Tales of Magic, Tales in Print: On the Genealogy of Fairy Tales and the Brothers Grimm* (2012), and the edited *Werewolf Histories* (2015). He is currently putting the finishing touches to *Werewolf Legends*, an edited volume in collaboration with Mirjam Mencej. He is also researching werewolf films, with articles in *Contemporary Legend* and *Gramarye*.

Gramarye

The Chichester Centre for Fairy Tales, Fantasy and Speculative Fiction

We hope you have enjoyed this 19th issue.

Please send any feedback to info@sussexfolktalecentre.org

Issue 20 of *Gramarye* will offer a similar mix of in-depth analysis, creative work, reviews, and commentary. To reserve your copy of *Gramarye* Issue 20, please contact Heather Robbins at h.robbins@chi.ac.uk.

We invite the submission of articles to peer review for inclusion in future issues of *Gramarye*. Your work should resonate with the main aim of the Centre, which is to provide writers and scholars from various disciplines with a forum to discuss folk narratives, fairy tales, and fantasy works, as independent genres and in terms of the resonances and dissonances between them and other cultural forms. Please refer to the Submission Guidelines opposite and send any queries to the Editorial Board at info@sussexfolktalecentre.org.

THE CHICHESTER CENTRE FOR FAIRY TALES AND FANTASY SPECULATIVE FICTION

Subscriptions to *Gramarye* are available at chi.ac.uk/scfff